Karolinum Press

Ivo Možný
Why So Easily ...
Some Family Reasons for the Velvet Revolution

VÁCLAV HAVEL SERIES

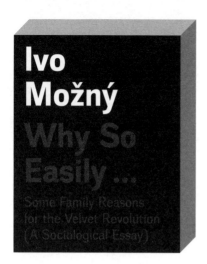

Ivo
Možný

Why So
Easily ...

Some Family Reasons
for the Velvet Revolution
(A Sociological Essay)

KAROLINUM PRESS

KAROLINUM PRESS is a publishing department of Charles University
Ovocný trh 560/5, 116 36 Prague 1, Czech Republic
www.karolinum.cz

Originally published in Czech as *Proč tak snadno. Některé rodinné důvody sametové revoluce. Sociologický esej*, Prague: SLON, 4th edition, 2022 (1991)

Cover and graphic design by 3.dílna
Set and printed in the Czech Republic by Karolinum Press
First English edition

Cataloging-in-Publication Data is available from the National Library
of the Czech Republic

ISBN 978-80-246-5315-0
ISBN 978-80-246-5316-7 (pdf)
ISBN 978-80-246-5317-4 (epub)

To Josef Škvorecký, author of *The Cowards*.

With great respect.

CONTENTS

Across the ponds the forest started to murmur, and as the shadow
of the summer clouds amply fills the hollow with its little town, and then
moves up the opposite slope, before halting for a long time beneath Kaňúr
on the Slovak border - seemingly motionless due to the great distance -
I have a premonition that suddenly everything will change: without us,
simply due to its nature, or due to the Earth's regular rotation.

Ludvík Vaculík, July 1982[1]

The theory of knowledge is a dimension of political theory because
the specifically symbolic power to improve the principles of the construction
of reality - in particular, social reality - is a major dimension of political
power.

Pierre Bourdieu

---

1 Transl. by Gerald Turner.

PREFACE TO THE THIRD EDITION

As I introduce this booklet to the reader for the third time, I cannot help but notice how dramatically the times are a-changing. The entire political landscape has changed from when I wrote my essay twenty years ago. Where are the old foreign travel permits[2], where is the hope I had that in spring I would manage to get my hands on a bicycle and that fridges might be available in the run up to Christmas? Where is the capitalism described by the Communist Party newspaper *Rudé právo* that we were destined not only to catch up with but to overtake, where are the women fighting for peace?! What's more, the priorities of the age are different. Who back then had heard of energy dependency, the global war on terrorism, the ominously rising sovereign debt and the creeping distaste for parliamentary democracy...? The readers themselves have changed. They no longer have to wait in an endless queue for an apartment, though they now are burdened by a mortgage. They buy a car before they've even had their first child, and no longer send their underlings to represent them so they can carry on building their weekend cottage, but instead find themselves wondering how they will pay the mortgage if their business closes down in the crisis... Why are people still buying this essay?

Twenty years ago I attempted to understand a society characterised by despotic socialism and explain some of the mechanisms that had allowed it to function successfully for so long. As this society becomes history, the old regime is being transformed before our very eyes into something from a fairy tale by the Brothers Grimm. Or perhaps a comic puppet show. On the stage, in front of the flimsy scenery, a series of characters enter jerkily: the Communist, the Dissident, the StB agent, the Independent, the Apparatchik... and in

---

2   *výjezdní doložka*, a document that had to be accompanied by the recommendation of an employer, school, military command or national committee: translator's note, henceforth t/n.

the background, of course, a crowd of extras playing the Ordinary People. "Where would I fit in?" you ask yourself. Well, you'd probably be Škrhola[3].

The protagonists of this puppet show must be cast carefully. If it were based in fact, there would be no one left in the group of extras. A large number of the Ordinary People over time played many different roles, sometimes simultaneously. In 1990, I learned that three of my best friends from the normalisation period (1970–80s) had been StB collaborators. One of these Agents was also a Dissident, one an Independent, and one a Communist. It goes without saying that all three were fundamentally decent people, punctilious professionals and upstanding intellectuals, and always had been. After all, the StB did not recruit rogues and kept well clear of nonentities. Instead, it blackmailed into submission people that enjoyed the respect of those around them.

This is all so difficult to understand from today's vantage point. For those who were not around at the time, the difficulty is compounded by the fact that the mega-narrative is so wonderfully logical, clear and compelling – not to speak of the fact that it is always so tempting to judge your parents. On the contrary, it is far more difficult to ask whether your own conduct does not include the same elements of opportunism by which our petty lives deal with the great movement of history, but now simply garbed in a flashier jacket. And for those who were there at the time, things remain difficult because the media fairy tale gets entangled in their own personal memories. The process of selective memory, with which we are all fortunately equipped, kicks in, since otherwise our inability to come to terms with our own past would drive us mad.

Our lives are lived in episodes and we can only understand them as a story. Each of these stories is at the same time constructed as an

---

3 A figure from puppet theatre a bit like Punch in English theatre, who represents the archetypal country bumpkin: t/n.

explanation – that is its hidden bonding agent. In order to make our explanation acceptable, or at least tolerable, not least to ourselves, we often employ somewhat convoluted but completely unconscious strategies involving the selective recall of lived episodes.

We also know that the story of our lives does not unfold in a wasteland. It needs its period scenery, i.e. the context in which it is narrated and in which it becomes comprehensible. Without a script we would be unable to piece together the dramas of our lives or replay them in our own memory, let alone recount them to others. However, once we begin to speak of these dramas and fables (and thus legitimise them) – once we attempt to communicate our story, even maybe to our loved ones – the background against which events are played out must be constructed in advance, clear and self-evident to all. Our story winds its way through the past, and this is a landscape our listeners did not figure in. Evoking the scenery of the past, that vanished context of our lives, is so difficult as to be impossible. No one is capable of fashioning such a expansive backdrop on their own. It is created by public discourse, to which our intimate discourses can but make reference. The background to the story of our lives is created by the media.

After every great coup, work begins on the construction of an overarching shared narrative of national history as if from scratch. Tearing down the old scenery is the first aspiration of every revolution, even of the most velvety variety. The new scenery is created quickly, because there must be a background from which narratives can detach themselves. The show must go on.

And thus emerge the lies of memory, the collective, national memory. However feeble and simplistic they may be as explanations, they do at least allow us to understand each other, which is a start. And as soon as the debate gets underway, an established version of the past is now indispensable. What we have before us today is this mainstream version of our national past.

However, one day there will have to be a reckoning with our shared past. This will not happen without a deconstruction of what are now valid and well established images from the recent history of the Czech nation. This is not the work of a few days and is a task for professional historians. It took the French until the late 1990s before Gallimard published the three-volume *Les Lieux de Mémoire*,[4] which confronts the media discourse with a polemical, nuanced image of the 1940s, beginning with the stories of the French during World War II and continuing into the turbulent years that followed. We lack such a monumental work of self-reflection.

And so for the third time I am launching this little booklet of mine, now twenty years old, into the world in the hope that it might ring bells in the minds of older readers, and indeed younger readers who, though not actors in the events described, view the narrative presented by the media as being suspiciously simple. It may help them frame better the question of how things actually were.

Of course, the answers that the essay from 1990 offers have themselves already been subsumed into history. This text was, I believe, the first attempt in this country to understand what had just taken place and why. I have not changed a word of the original text. Now that we all know what happened over the following twenty years, we have the opportunity of learning from this text how everything that followed actually began. In this respect, I myself feel the main weakness or shortcoming of the text is that it did not pay more attention to the mechanisms of power and coercion in the old regime. These are age-old mechanisms, and it seems to me that a better explanation of how they work could have provided powerful inspiration for understanding the whole of this history up to the present day. I took it for granted, much to my regret, that the pernicious entanglement of politics, economics, governance and knowledge was dead and buried. Part of the optimism that followed in the wake of the revolution

4   Pierre Nora et al.: *Les lieux de mémoire*, vols. 1 to 3, Paris : Gallimard 1997.

was of course the assumption that this essay was simply a first crack at things, to be followed by more nuanced attempts, since the theme would without doubt appeal to many younger sociologists and historians. To them, too, I would like to dedicate this latest edition.

Brno, 25 May 2009   Ivo Možný

PREFACE TO THE SECOND EDITION
What we didn't know ten years ago

Those unfortunates who choose not to look back on the path of history lest they happen to see a grizzly bear, often find themselves wailing *too late, too late*, as anyone will know who is familiar with the song by Vodňanský about bears and tourists[5].

Having said that, to present my own text to readers ten years after it was written during the tumultuous years of 1989 and 1990, when things did indeed seem a little simpler, smacks of masochism. Perhaps it would be a better idea to display the general's wisdom after the battle, the benefit of hindsight on which the media discourse is also based, and rely on what sustains politicians, namely, the fact that no one reads old texts. It suffices that outdated political analyses will one day serve the needs of historians, who will dissect the language of such analyses and incorporate them into historical narratives that cast a merciless eye over the naivety of yesteryear. This is perhaps why sociologists do not publish their collected works: on the rare occasion a publisher is tempted to break this rule, it is only after the great sociologist in question is safely six feet under.

But a constitutive part of our lived experience is the original naivety that led to us having to acquire that experience. Those who are never in the wrong may be right, but never experience anything: they remain rooted in one place. Society evolves because the population as a whole is never right. It is for this reason that history is so vivid.

We might therefore view the purpose of republishing a ten-year-old sociological text as being to remind us of what we did not know ten years ago, and to shed light on where and how we were naive. Before my readers begin the process of reflection for themselves, I would like to point out one or two examples of where I myself was naive.

---

5 *Grizzly* by Jan Vodňanský and Petr Skoumal: t/n.

Interestingly, this will not include the Postscript at the end of my essay, in which I declare the adage *Trust others!* to be most important for the success of the social reconstruction that was to follow. Back then, when I added that this would not be any easier than it had been adhering to the admonishment to *Live in truth!* under the old regime, I myself had no idea how much harder it would be in reality. The trust deficit I wrote of at the start of transformation keeps on growing. What we have achieved over the last ten years can be calculated using various criteria that offer very different results. Measured by the number of Czechs taking holidays in Italy or Spain or the availability of juicy tangerines in the lead-up to Christmas, we are a million miles from life as it used to be. However, measured by the level of mutual trust, something that gives great cause for concern is that we have not moved on one jot. One is tempted to say that the level of general paranoia has actually increased, though this would not be quite true: these days it is simply served up on a plate along with the morning newspaper.

And yet the fact remains: unless the level of trust rises in this country, we will build neither capitalism nor civil society. If anyone is still in any doubt as to my assertion that trust is the key to progress as measured by quality of life, let them hear it for themselves from the author of the sociological best seller *The End of History*, Francis Fukuyama, who at the end of the 1990s wrote a book on this theme called simply *Trust* (1994). We are in full agreement. And by the end of the year there will be a third such text, since Piotr Sztompka is shortly to have a study entitled *Trust* published by Cambridge University Press.

The injunction to *trust others*, taken in isolation, is of course naive. Not even the most irresponsible mother would advise her little daughter to *trust others* without adding: But only those you know – never accept a lift from a strange man, even (especially) if he offers you sweets! As I was finalising the text of *Why So Easily...* in 1990, I wondered whether I shouldn't change the title to *Build trust!*. But

I realised that I wouldn't be helping anyone that way, and might end up simply pandering to a reader too lazy to think for themselves. The more attentive reader will find their own path between the two variants of the same adage for themselves. The only way to build trust in the other is to trust the other. Without this modest investment I can't even buy a sandwich. If I say: "I'm not handing you my money until I see the sandwich", I'll be met with: "Bugger off, I'm not handing you this sandwich until I see my money!", and we will find ourselves in a standoff that has no solution. *Build trust!* implies *Show trust!*, and that means beginning with the other – no other route exists.

Of course, we must be on our guard against the strange man offering sweets. For many years we had no choice but to pay heed to primitive wisdom: only from your uncle, he's family. But beware of strangers! It is precisely because the population of the countries of despotic socialism were deprived for generations of the opportunity to cultivate the difficult skill of making prudent investments of trust on the open market over and above the circle of their inherited network of acquaintances that there have been so many bankruptcies, complete with next-day shame and regret. It is telling that it was in Albania, the country that of all European states remains closest to being a clan-based society, that several huge financial pyramid schemes, which exploited the blind faith of inexperienced Albanians as they welcomed capitalism, enjoyed such devastating success – to the point where both the currency and the government collapsed.

We all make mistakes. In an open society based on individual responsibility, we settle the bill and write off the loss (and collect the settlement based on the insurance premium we have been sensibly paying in order to cover losses), just as we write off those who have betrayed our trust. We don't stop there, nor does business based on the capital of trust end there. (If anyone quits, it is the party that has broken faith).

This is always supposing we don't make too many such mistakes. If we do, we declare bankruptcy promptly, divide up what is left among our creditors in order to satisfy them at least in part, and find a way of making a living doing something for which we have greater talent, though it be considerably less lucrative. We take full responsibility for our mistakes. We may have lost credit, but we have not lost face.

How naive, you say, having experienced the first ten years of the way that trust is negotiated in this country. What I didn't see coming ten years ago was the overall loss of social responsibility as the natural consequence of socialisation in a state colonised by clans. And I did not foresee what the atrophy of a sense of responsibility would entail.

Perhaps what I lacked back then was a term for *responsibility* in my sociological discourse. The very word appeared to me to belong to psychologists, if not to the language of normative ethics. However, it has its own place in the sociological vision of the world, as does the concept of trust. Sociology found no use for the latter concept until the 1970s, when it was taken up by Bourdieu and Granovetter.

The concept of responsibility was introduced into the language of normative ethics by European capitalism. *Responsibility* occupies top place among all the civic virtues, since without it, none of the others would exist. It is not individualism, as often claimed, but the successful combination of individualism and responsibility that gave rise to societies of the Western cultural circle, so dynamic that they eventually aspired (naively it goes without saying) to put an end to historical disputes over the perfect social system, having found it (or so they believed).

If it is true that sociology did not arise along with industrialism and the open society as its legitimising self-reflection merely by coincidence, the concept of *responsibility* in its glossary of terms should be present from the very start. Which indeed it is. The problem was mine: ten years ago I had not read enough Durkheim.

For Durkheim, one of the founding fathers of sociology, individualism was the thorniest intellectual problem when interpreting the society in which he lived and which he was convinced could be explained *sociologically*. He believed it should be possible to explain human behaviour as arising from social pressures that were objective to such an extent that they had the nature of objects. He successfully defended this claim against the psychologism and organicism that was popular at that time, thus earning his place in the pantheon of thinkers who had attempted to understand social mechanisms. However, how are we to understand the phenomenon of individualism if at the same time we claim that we cannot liberate the way we act from our embeddedness in social institutions? Is individualism merely a chimera, an approach to life virtually never instantiated?

For Durkheim it is not, nor was it for any of the social thinkers of his time. Individualism was too important a part of the emancipation of the middle class, to which sociologists inescapably belong. In *Suicide* (1897), the concept served Durkheim merely as an explanation of the weakness or fragility of what was otherwise the self-confident, robust bourgeois society of his time: he assumed that social groups that were more individualistic were likely to be associated with higher suicide rates. However, in his essay "The Division of Labour in Society" (1893), and above all in "Individualism and the Intellectuals" (1898)[6], he explains the positive role individualism plays in the constitution of modern societies.

The key to understanding this role lies in the relationship between individualism and responsibility. Or, to be more precise, in the identification of individualism with responsibility. Durkheim draws on the concept of individualism we find in Kant and Rousseau and in the *Declaration of Human Rights*. It is this individualism that has become "the basis of our moral catechism...", since it works with a concept of the human being as "sacred in the ritual sense of that

6   Emile Durkheim: L'Individualisme et les intellectuels. *Revue Bleu*, vol. 4, no. 10 (1898), 7–13. Cited in R. N. Bellah (ed.): *Emile Durkheim on Morality and Society*. Chicago: University of Chicago Press 1973

word". Individualism has "permeated our institutions and our morals" and become a modern faith in which man is "... both worshipper and at the same time god". Durkheim explains what he means when he speaks of individualism as the cult of secular society and of the man who believes in this cult as follows:

"The cult of which he is at once both object and follower does not address itself to the particular being that constitutes himself and carries his name, but to the human person, wherever it is to be found, and in whatever form it is incarnated... Individualism thus understood is the glorification not of the self, but of the individual in general. Its motive force is not egoism but sympathy for all that is human, a wider pity for all sufferings, for all human miseries, a more ardent desire to combat and alleviate them, a greater thirst for justice." (Durkheim 1898)

The grand narrative of Western European individualism is above all a narrative of responsibility: first and foremost the full acceptance of responsibility for the quality of one's own life; and secondly for the quality of one's own society. One without the other is not possible (something we Czechs should have some experience of). Viewed from this perspective, Man is responsible for what he has made of his life, and this includes what he has done to make it possible to generate something worthwhile in his society from human life.

If we place what passes in this country these days for individualism alongside what we have said above, we obtain an insight into one of the great misunderstandings of the post-revolutionary years. The Czech nation arrived at freedom as a blind man arrives at a violin: it simply fell into its lap. Our great-grandfathers, who had been working hard to achieve civic emancipation from the middle of the last century, have been largely forgotten. Fifty years of humiliation in an authoritarian society is too long a break for the delicate fabric of moral responsibility that is buried in the family casket for better times not to rot.

"Durkheimian individualism is a sociological concept, which is used to explain the experience by individuals of an external and constraining moral reality (a 'social fact'), through which individuals understand their world and within which they feel obliged to act."[7]

Individualism in the Czech Republic has run wild. It has lost its sense of responsibility, without which it is inevitably becoming a sad caricature of itself. The pride the individual takes in the fact that all of his actions are morally justifiable has gone missing, and without this all that remains of individualism is expedient utilitarianism and unscrupulous selfishness. However, this is a weak cement for a complex society with a developed division of labour and mutual dependency. This is not a question of normative ethics but of sociology.

Most Czechs do not believe that someone could sincerely believe in God. And so few of them are willing to base their actions on the assumption that their fellow human beings, whether believers or non-believers, will treat them in accordance with the Ten Commandments. Not even the bride that stands before the altar. The possibility of divorce cannot be ruled out, and some infidelity or other must be reckoned with. In a secularised world the same applies to all cooperation. The ever-present possibility of deceit and duplicity has become the unspoken assumption behind every cooperative strategy. And every act of cooperation must assume that the cooperating partner is basing their actions on the same premise. In the end it kind of works, though such a degree of necessary mutual vigilance imposes high costs on the quality and thus the productivity of all cooperation. So high, in fact, that we Czechs are not competitive in an open world. And a foreigner hesitates to enter this poisonous milieu, where they must assume that the party they are dealing with regards universal mutual treachery to be the basis of the functioning of the system.

---

7   Bill Jordan, Marcus Redley, Simon James: *Putting the Family First.* London: UCL Press 1994, 30.

In one way Czech society is unlucky. It has reopened its doors to the civilisation from which it arose, just at the moment this civilisation is itself experiencing difficulties. On the one hand, the imperative of technological progress and the logic of the rational layout of the universe and market pressures work against what they themselves emerged from, namely, the Protestant ethic of frugality and deferred gratification. However, along with the Protestant ethic, these mechanisms are beginning to undermine fatally the entire system of ethical norms associated with it, even though it was only thanks to them that they arose and it is upon them that they remain dependent. A relativist ethic of "anything goes" emerges. Moral reality as a social fact loses its clarity and with it its significance as a practical regulator of behaviour – not for everyone, but at a dangerous rate for the stupider strata of the population at least.

On the other hand, Western civilisation is facing unprecedented cultural pressure from huge waves of immigration, which in terms of numbers is slowly becoming the movement of entire peoples. These days one in every five, sometimes four, inhabitants of German cities is an immigrant, and across the Atlantic, especially in the south and west of the United States, there are cities where ethnic minorities now comprise the majority.

Immigration is caused not only by the vast disparities in the living standards of the developed and developing countries, but also by the demographic vacuum spreading throughout our civilisation. A child is the quintessence of deferred utility, and the atrophy of the Protestant ethic is opening up a space for what would at one time been regarded as a completely deranged question: why have children at all? For several decades now, the ten wealthiest countries in the world have reported birth rates below the net reproduction rate (and the Czech Republic, though far from being as rich and productive, is joining them in this respect). A demographic vacuum is being created and this, via the mechanism of unintended consequence, is inducing immigration.

Both of these pressures on the civilisational base of Western societies stand side by side: on the one hand, the moral insecurity of the West; on the other, the clan ethics of immigrant ethnicities, searching in vain within such insecurity for support for their assimilation into new civilisational conditions.

The same applies to us. Overnight we have collectively become immigrants of the open society of the West. We, too, have introduced into capitalism the ethic of a clan society that does not work here, causes us huge problems, and makes the West wary of opening itself up to us and multiplying its own problems, of which it already has more than enough.

However, Western civilisation has one critical advantage over us: it has responsible elites. Of course, it would be naive to cleave to illusions of the incorruptibility of the political, economic and cultural elites in European states, which are at present carefully considering whether to admit us into the Union. Many of them also emerged relatively recently from chaos and disruption. If we look where Spain, Finland, Greece, Italy, France, Austria and Germany were and what they looked like just half a century ago, it offers us hope. However, even in these most stable countries there were and are members of the elite who succumb to the desire for power and riches and fail in their mission. *Auri sacra fames*, or the cursed hunger for gold, said the ancient Romans, and that was a mature civilisation!

But let us not overlook a fundamental difference. Such aberrant conduct on the part of Western elites is always a clear and distinguishable *failure*: a lapse from the norm, not behaviour that can be expected because it is customary in the region. The difference is difficult to make out, especially if viewed from afar. This is another reason why so many Czechs are convinced that, when all is said and done, theft is ubiquitous[8]. Ok, so theft goes on everywhere. However,

---

8   *Všude se krade*, a Czech adage similar in universalising intent as *Kdo nekrade, okrádá rodinu*, or He who does not steal, robs his own family: t/n.

it is on a different scale and under far greater restrictive pressure of moral reality. Individualism here is indeed a sociological concept, explaining the experience of the individual with a moral reality that is external to him and binding upon him (a "social fact"), and by means of which he perceives the world and *feels obliged to act*, even if this is not always strictly in accordance with said moral reality.

Our problem is not individualism, but the atrophy of moral reality. The variability of cultural and moral norms does not mean their absence. Without my being aware of it, in what I wrote ten years ago I was attempting to peer through the official rhetoric and cynical pearls of demotic wisdom and distinguish behind them the concealed framework of morality in the old society: it was there. It was there, even in the confused relationship with the counter-elitism of the Chartists, in the quiet desperation at the prevailing circumstances, even in fumbling attempts to build at least a casual network of trustworthy friends, with whom we might share a kind of moral reality, even though it was not – and could not be – the subject of public debate. I touched upon all of this indirectly, even though I did not recognise in my naivety how significant it was to an understanding of the world I was attempting to explain.

The need to justify one's actions in relation to principles that transcend the instinct for self-preservation seems immanent to humankind: all known societies believe in some god, even if it is not always personified. Rather than the absence of such norms, what we face these days is their inadequacy in the light of the new demands being made on the complexity and sophistication of the societal division of labour, demands that were suddenly imported into our society as being the attributes of an open society. Clan morality, which has functioned here as the moral reality for half a century, is incapable of meeting these demands.

The manifest desperation engendered by the rickety morality of our political and economic elites, which is beginning to permeate the whole of society, harbours both hope and hazard. Hope that this desperation is both a sign and proof of the existence of a moral framework within which theft as the most effective form of privatisation, and politics as clan-based horse-trading over kickbacks and privileges, are both deemed totally unjustifiable. Hazard in that it is also a sign of envy and impatience.

Each of us must deal with envy on our own: it is a character flaw. We may be assisted in this endeavour by Bertrand Russell's observation that socialism is institutionalised envy, as well as our own bitter experience of what envy does when it becomes state ideology. As for impatience, this deserves greater understanding: impatience in the pursuit of the good often aspires to virtue. This is a mistake, within which a dangerous trap is concealed on the social level. If democratic institutions are to function well, they must necessarily also sometimes function poorly. They are not based on consent: they are tools for balancing dissent and diversity, they are a transitory, continually renewed equilibrium between conflicting interests. This makes them dynamic, but it also means that they move forward by means of trial and error. Democracy cannot be better than its citizens, and is similar to them in that it, too, finds it difficult to learn other than from its mistakes. And so if we were to view the existence of mistakes as a fundamental flaw, the next step might involve looking for something better than democracy, rather than trying to correct its mistakes. This next step in the cultivation of distaste for the failings of democracy marks the start of an appreciation for the benefits of dictatorship. The Oxford sociologist and great friend of the Czech Republic, Stein Ringen, wrote the following:

"Real democracies are necessarily imperfect. This is an exceedingly elementary observation, but also one of great importance for the understanding of democracy, and that appreciation again is of great importance for democracy itself. If we want democracy to be without flaws, we shall be disappointed. If we want democracy to produce prosperity and order over night, we shall be disillusioned. If disappointment and disillusion are prevailing sentiments among citizens, the vitality of democracy will be undermined. If, instead, we remember that democracy is predominantly about liberty, we can appreciate its greatness in spite of imperfection. Democracy delivers liberty, and it delivers more, but it does not do everything and it does not do everything at once.

Perfection is a dangerous idea: it is the idea that there is an end towards which history is, or should be, moving; it is an authoritarian idea, an idea alien to the spirit of democracy."[9]

What we were unaware of ten years ago was not the advantages of an open society: oddly enough we knew all about them. It was just how imperfect such a society was. Among the illusions I have had to bid farewell to since the first edition of this book is that we would be sufficiently patient to regard democracy's natural tendency to make mistakes as a natural quality, which it owes to its dynamism. We did not know to what extent the authoritarian idea of perfection was implanted within us. We did not suspect just how many politicians would shamelessly make a living out of cultivating such a distaste for the failings of democracy that many of those who do not have the patience for the slow slog forward would turn and face the past.

Perhaps the text that follows, on how the old regime, which aspired to perfection, was overwhelmed by citizens who availed themselves of its imperfections almost to perfection, and in doing so eventually overcame it without actually seeking to, will help us understand the meaning of the imperfection of democracy that today provokes in us fury, apathy or grief, depending on the kind of person we are. We slipped off the shackles of socialism so easily because capitalism was waiting for us within it. We are finding it difficult to get the hang of capitalism, because our own had been prepared in socialism.

Our capitalism reeks of the cauldron in which it was cooked. Not by the old structures. By all of us.

9   Stein Ringen: *Citizens, Families, and Reform.* Oxford: Clarendon Press 1997, 2.

Perhaps Moses will not have to spend all of forty years leading us through the desert, merely to ensure that only those who are not branded as slaves reach the promised land of an open society. Average life expectancy has increased since then, and these days it would be more like seventy years. Be merciful, o Lord.

Kulířov, July 1999   Ivo Možný

PREFACE TO THE FIRST EDITION

Unlike history, sociology has a duty to attempt an explanation of historical events before they are removed from the agenda of the day.

It should also speak to those of whom it is writing, and not simply write for an audience of the initiated.

However, once the author leaves the safe space of professional guidelines and becomes embroiled in the reality of pressing interests, they risk demeaning themself.

Perhaps one form of defence is the essay form. However, Šalda[10] set the bar unfeasibly high and created an excessively close link between the essay and literature. Nevertheless, if we look to the Anglo-Saxon tradition and regard the essay as embodying the reflections of an expert, who renounces neither intuition nor even occasional displays of intellectual playfulness, notwithstanding the fact it might result in an overly personal perspective, then we have what we need. I am, of course, aware that my claims are somewhat exaggerated in places. However, I am convinced that I am exaggerating only the true claims. I am aware, too, that I risk being catastrophically wrong. However, I believe that as far as research is concerned, the worst enemy of a good explanation is not a bad explanation, but the absence of any alternative explanation.

It is for this reason that I have permitted myself this attempt at a sociological essay.

Wassenaar, January 1991 Ivo Možný

---

10 F. X. Šalda, 1867–1937, literary critic, journalist and writer, sometimes regarded as the founder of modern Czech art criticism: t/n.

Chapter One

Why so late?

Questions regarding the nature of what has become known as the Velvet Revolution are only now beginning to be asked. Of the many such questions being raised, for our purposes the simplest three are also the most interesting, namely: Why did it take us so long before we opted for change? How come the subsequent collapse was so fast and smooth? And who actually participated on those crowded public squares? It is only after we have answered these three questions that we can cautiously pose a fourth: *What lies in store for us now?*

Why did it take us so long before we opted for change?

Jan Ruml wrote the following in an illegal edition of the newspaper *Lidové Noviny*:

"Let's be honest. It is taking a long time for our society to wake up. Basically, society is dully accepting of the direct, shameless provocation practiced by the regime... Forty years of effort on the part of the ignorant to ravage all areas of national life, along with the systematic construction of consumerist socialist chauvinism, has had the desired effect. The vast majority of the population more or less participated in these processes. And so when someone criticises this system, in truth they are criticising themselves."

These acerbic words were written shortly after the official celebrations of the founding of independent Czechoslovakia on 28 October 1989. The cynical and Orwellian move on the part of the central committee of the Communist Party, by means of which what had been "nationalisation day" was transformed in 1988 into a state holiday celebrating the founding of the republic, was a slap in the face of decency and an attack on the integrity of every citizen. This was the second time the opposition organised its own, unofficial celebration on a different day in protest against the hypocritical attempt on the part of the ruling party to appropriate the memory of a state it had destroyed. The opposition hoped that by organising such an event it would create the space for the expression of mass dissatisfaction with the prevailing situation.

However, expectations of dissent were once again dashed. Within the whole of Czechoslovakia, only about 37,000 people (according to Ruml's own estimate) had the courage – or rather, in the spirit of his words cited above, found within themselves the strength of spirit – to confront face-to-face their own shame and responsibility and make plain to the state that it could no longer count on their consent, even though this consent had taken the form of silence. Something had been organised in Prague, but almost nothing in smaller towns and cities.[11] And yet so little was being asked of the participants: to put on a thick sweater and raincoat and turn up at a square. If enough people turned up, the likelihood of being sanctioned was minimal. But given a population of fifteen million (ok, let's say ten million adults), forty thousand people spread across all the town squares in the entire republic, with all due respect for their solidarity, is a tiny minority. If these demonstrations were translated into the results of an election, then the opposition would have won but 0.4% of the vote.

No one in politics can expect to be taken seriously with such little active support behind them. It is no wonder that the State Security Services took it upon themselves to organise the coup. Two weeks before 17 November 1989, confronted by this reality, the prospects of our opposition did not look promising. Ruml's disappointment was understandable and justified. Our immediate neighbours had already brought down the Berlin Wall, but the situation in this country looked grim.

"What is a lot and what is a little? How many people does it take on a public protest for their leaders to understand that they must stand down? In East Germany there were hundreds of thousands on the streets, maybe even a million. A million people who realised almost overnight whither the path lay to freedom and civil society. Meanwhile, in Czechoslovakia millions of people burdened with shopping bags are wandering around in a fenced

---

11 "When my friends need a wash, they have to come to Prague," my younger son observed bitterly regarding the situation in Brno during the January disturbances. (The Communist police used water cannons against the opposition demonstrations in Prague: t/n.)

country almost aimlessly. The wooden poles on which the barbed wire is fastened are rotting and the barricades are falling to the ground. Eventually there will be nobody keeping guard over us and we will discover with horror that, through no fault of our own, we too are free." (Ruml, 1989)

Things weren't quite that bad. A week later the squares were packed. In Prague alone, with its population of one million, around 800,000 people came to Letná Plain. Small towns and villages joined in, and the State Security Service completely lost control.

Within two months Václav Havel was president and the entire oppressive system lay in ruins.

However, this new political reality did not leap into the world like Minerva from the head of Jupiter. The ground had been laid by countless indiscernible social movements, which came together in a text that made sense, but that no one could yet read in full: "every era carries in its womb a child in whom one may not only place one's hopes, but through whom and with whom it would be possible to go on living", writes Bohumil Hrabal in *Inzerát na dům, ve kterém už nechci bydlet*[12]. In this country the child had been waiting to be born for some time. Of course, with typically Czech caution we sat in our seats waiting for the moment when history would pass through the carriage of the almost empty train of socialism calling out: "Everyone disembark, the journey ends here!"

Unlike the Bulgarians and Romanians, however, subsequent developments suggest that Czech society was already fully primed to follow a different path.

But with difficulties greater than had appeared at first glance. Both the state of readiness and the difficulties were based on previous developments: Ruml was bang on the mark. And both were by now distinguishable.

---

[12] English translation Bohumil Hrabal: *Mr. Kafka and Other Tales from the Time of the Cult*, transl. Paul Wilson, New York: New Directions 2015.

For the purposes of a sociological analysis, an essay I wrote about six months earlier than this article will serve us well. I had had the text in my head for several years. However, since there were no outlets where I might publish it, I didn't even find the time to write it. Until, that is, a conference on functional analysis that took place in November 1989 provided an ideal opportunity and motivation.[13] Now might be a good time to read it just as it was written. (The reader who is not interested in sociological theory can skip parts 1 and 2.) The text both reflects upon and unwittingly reflects the period in which it was written. Inasmuch as I was mistaken back then, it is worth making the effort to demonstrate this today, since then we will have to find another explanation for some of the social phenomena taking place before our very eyes. And if, on the contrary, things were as they are described below, then we should not really be surprised by how things are today.

13 The existence of samizdat activities at the close of the post-totalitarian systems suited the establishment in a sense. It channelled dissatisfaction underground and enabled the elite to ignore a competing vision of reality, since it did not have to enter into a public discourse with it. However, if the apparatchiks were approached publicly, they now lacked the power to control the debate in such a way that they would have their opponent fired from work and professionally silenced. With Gorbachev's Russia at their backs, this was not the time.
So I did not offer this text to Alan and Petrusek for the *Sociologický obzor* (Sociological Horizon, a samizdat journal), but to Potůček for the proceedings of an upcoming conference on functional analysis in Moravský Krumlov, where in any case we all met as a legitimate theory section of the Czech Sociological Association. And in September, just after its publication in the legally published proceedings of this conference (Potůček and Szomolányiová 1989), I sent this text for publication to the journal *Sociológia*, which was not the most carefully policed journal, but by now a completely official forum for Marxist-Leninist sociology, a journal whose contents the establishment could not ignore: the ladies criticised in the article could hardly overlook its existence. However, their reaction, which I was really looking forward to, I never saw: history worked more quickly than our polygraphers.
However, it would be just as possible to formulate the questions asked within the context of sociological macro- and micro-theory within that of functionalism, as indeed I tried later (in a lecture for the Inter-University Centre in Dubrovník in April 1990), or political science (Proceedings of the IVth World Congress for Soviet and East European Studies, Harrogate July 1990). I wrote a commentary on the original essay that ended up being longer than what it was commenting on in Wassenaar, where I spent the academic year 1990–1991 as a fellow-in-residence of the Netherlands Institute for Advanced Study. I would like to avail myself of this opportunity to thank the Royal Netherlands Academy of Arts and Sciences.

THE CATCH IN THE FUNCTIONAL ANALYSIS OF THE FAMILY

(An essay written in spring 1989)

He who does not steal, robs his family.

A Czech popular saying

... analytical distinctions which do not take account of commonsense interpretations of social reality (but instead use simply what is accepted as common sense in sociology) are generally misleading.

David Silverman

1.

The family is one of the few social institutions in Czechoslovakia that cannot complain of a lack of functional analysis. The same cannot be said of sociological research into the process of automation, the business collective, youth, social homogenisation, value orientation, or way of life, just to select at random from the most prominent topics of the past years.

In Czechoslovakia, a Marxist sociology of the family was drawn to functional analysis for pragmatic and ideological reasons. From the pragmatic perspective, the functional approach made it possible to organise very diverse material. Data on birth rates, marriage, abortion and divorce collected by demographers, data on sexual behaviour collected by sexologists, the results of time-use research, intergenerational studies of educational and professional mobility, traditional speculations on changes to the internal organisation of the family, promiscuity and monogamy, the normative ideas of pedagogues regarding intergenerational relationships and the functional cooperation of parents and schools in the process of education, feminist demands for emancipation and socio-economic analyses of the female employment rate, theories of social formation and the constitution of class consciousness in the process of socialisation within the family... all this, and much more. The functional approach made it easy to classify and organise the entire confused agenda of social matrimoniology.

And, in addition, to present and propagate said agenda. This brings us to another pragmatic reason why functional analysis was so favoured by this discipline. The sociology of the family has the dubious honour of attracting the interest of a non-specialist public. Everyone understands the family. And functional analysis enjoys similar "luck": everyone knows that the word "function" refers to "the purpose that something serves". The most important Czech sociological studies of the family written over the last few decades were more a way of informing, educating and influencing an educated readership, rather than a development of theory and a way of expanding our cognitive horizons. They endorsed and promoted a new, socialist concept of the family. The functional approach was easy to understand and therefore well suited to the purpose of popularisation. Explaining to a lay audience the purpose or role of an object was sufficient to satisfy their intuitively teleological perception of the universe.

However, this simplified functional analysis was attractive not only for practical, but also ideological reasons. Most research being conducted into the sociology of the family over the last few decades implicitly or explicitly pursued the noble aim of taking arms against a hostile ideology. In this polemical struggle, Marxist sociology embodied two levels of abstraction. On the one hand, it dealt with the residua of capitalism in the public consciousness in the most general sense, the residua that the family reproduced through socialisation. On the other, it tackled "family ideology" in the narrower sense of the word, i.e. familiarism, a worldview in which the family is the axis and centre of the universe of the individual and the life of society, and in which the wellbeing of the family is the lodestar of all effort. The familiarist approach was long deemed a distinct threat to socialist society, and Marxist sociology, deeming it to be a "petty-bourgeois" approach to life, felt a professional responsibility for its suppression.

Under these circumstances, functional analysis was deemed the most appropriate polemical strategy in the ideological struggle. By deploying functional analysis, sociology was able to show that the family did not exist "for its own sake", but that it always served society as an irreplaceable social tool. It was important in the production of a future workforce, the socialisation of children in the social values of the ruling class, assisting the individual in the event of a life crisis, taking care of incapable, old or handicapped members of the family, providing for the redistribution and ultimately the creation of economic values, etc. What had been the original revolutionary radicalism weakened during the development of real socialism, and the claim that the state would take over most of these functions as soon as possible faded into the background. By the early 1970s, no one seriously questioned the importance of the family vis-à-vis the discharge of many social tasks in socialist society. However, the path to this state of affairs was long and tortuous, and will be examined later on.

2.

Although the functional approach in the sociology of the family primarily served the non-epistemic needs of the time, it nevertheless remained functional, with all the advantages and disadvantages of this theory of social reality. As an explicative principle it could not eliminate any of its weaknesses. It was in its interest to address head-on the well known critique of functionalism: calling itself Marxist did not render it immune to attack from within a specialist context.

So now let us review the main objections raised to functionalism and examine to what extent they apply to the case in question.

A good starting point is the effective presentation of these objections by Cohen (1968). Cohen distinguishes three categories of criticism: logical, substantive and ideological.

"The main logical arguments against functionalism are that it encourages teleological explanation, that it suggests hypotheses which are untestable, that it demands a level of scientific inquiry which does not exist in sociology and, finally, that it inhibits comparison... The chief substantive criticisms of functionalism are these: it overemphasises the normative element in social life; it minimises the importance of social conflict at the expense of social solidarity; it stresses the harmonious nature of social systems; and, finally, it fails to account for social change and even treats this as abnormal."

Ideological criticism adds to this litany of objections the fact that "functionalism encourages or reflects a conservative bias." The first thing we would say in defence of functionalism is that there exist many varieties to which the criticisms listed above are sometimes, and sometimes not, applicable. The criticism of its teleological explanation and normative deviations apply to that branch of sociological functionalism deriving from Malinowsky and is clearly inapplicable. Malinowsky's functionalism is based on needs, in the first instance the biological needs of the human being as living creature. Malinowsky sees social needs as coordinating and communicating needs arising from the fact that in order to attain their primary needs, humans must necessarily associate and cooperate.

However, Czech matrimoniological functionalism does not draw on this source. It is based, rather, on a kind of autonomy of social needs. These are embedded in norms based on social consensus, such as we find in Parsons.[14] In Parson's view, the state or society also

14 A quick reminder of Parsons' approach: "According to Parsons, values and norms must be understood analytically as independent of any special group or role. Roles and groups are 'particularistic' in a given system, they are the roles of specific individuals and groups with a particular participation in a role. But within a given system, values and norms are 'universalistic',

needs, expects and rightly demands from the family things that are often not only in conflict with the immediate needs of the family and its members, but which cannot even be derived from these needs in any logical way. These needs are justified by "social goals" and "generally shared values". However, the layperson may overlook and the propagandist ignore what should not have escaped the attention of sociologists, namely, that there is a logical flaw here: a value may be declared "generally shared" even though it is not a value for any of those sharing it. It is only when they have been convinced from outside that they act in accordance with it, so as not to differ from those around them. The value introduced into this circular logic starts to be perceived as a necessity (most often as a "societal necessity", which makes verification on the basis of a realised benefit impossible), and outside of this circular logic the goal thus set does not need any further justification: after all, everyone shares it.

In addition, this is not evident to the senses and cannot be empirically proven. A second logical weakness of functionalism emerges: its hypotheses are untestable. If, for instance, it is claimed that "society" needs a high birth rate and that the function of the family is to meet this demand by creating and bringing up the appropriate number of children, this is not explained as an expression of the natural needs of families (struggling with housing and other problems), nor as a higher-order need, e.g. the need to prepare for the future in the sphere of care for the old and disabled, but simply on the basis of the fulfilment of state policy, which is to maintain and increase the size of the population. This goal is open to explanation, but not, however, through recourse to the functionalist approach,

i.e. they are not specific either to situations or to functions (as opposed to goals), and are independent of the inner differentiation of the system. Roles are controlled by the normative necessities of groups. The behaviour of a group as a subsystem of broader systems is controlled by institutionalised norms specifying how each type of group must behave given its place in the system. And norms are legitimised and thus in a normative sense controlled by the values institutionalised in society." (Klofáč, Tlustý 1965) which now becomes teleological. (Such an explanation could draw, for instance, on the army's need for a particular number of recruits, or the inertia of the economy, which requires a larger labour force in order to keep growing, or the power of the social groups that have an interest in seeing these measures enacted.) And so the social need cannot be tested empirically and cannot be replaced by another need when an opportune occasion arises. (In the case we have been discussing this might involve a denatalist policy as a goal and social value declared at the moment when those who formulate social rhetoric would prefer to see less pressure on schools, apartments and jobs. We were witness to the first variant in the mid-1970s and the second is emerging at present. Likewise, the teleological arguments surrounding universal women's employment and the collective education of children in day-care centres have changed and continue to change.)

The last instance of a Czech teleological explanation is the "socialist way of life" and the lower-level, more targeted goals derived therefrom, such as collectivism, optimism, egalitarianism, guaranteed safety and a universal concept of security, state paternalism, etc. On the basis of these values, further operationalised partial goals are extracted, which, however, are already being transformed under the influence of reality, eventually into their antitheses. Here are a few examples of such values and their antitheses. Only the state builds and allocates apartments *versus* support for the construction of private housing leading eventually to the prevalence of private over state-owned flats; labourers should enjoy the same pay as skilled engineers *versus* small income differences as a problem of wage-levelling; the collective upbringing of all children in day-centres from the earliest age *versus* the attainment of long-term maternity leave; collective holidaymaking with a Revolutionary Trade Union Movement (ROH) voucher for all *versus* private weekend cottages – all of these have at some time or other been functional in the development of the socialist way of life. However, in the face of feedback, operational changes undermine the initial values. An unequivocal enthusiasm for collectivism and egalitarianism subsides, along with the concomitant feelings of security and optimism, though the inertia of the functional explanation persists.

The problem, of course, is not that social goals *qua* teleological explanation are changing. The very existence of change would controvert the criticism of functionalism's inability to explain social change – if, that is, we were to find such explanations in Czech sociological analyses of the family. Instead, we are forced to concede that all analyses of the function of the family in socialist society conceive it as universal and, inasmuch as we are talking of a socialist society, ahistorical.

This ahistoricity is already presupposed by the consensual basis of the normative conception of functionalism in this country: how could sociologists analyse movement if, from their chosen perspective, they were unable to see any conflict? After all, as every Marxist knows, it is conflict that is supposed to be the driving force of social development. All functions and the needs derived therefrom are presented as universal social needs of the "whole of society". The four basic functions of the family (or indeed the three or ten basic functions, if we divide them into sub-functions like Tyskzka [1974]: the number is of no importance) are deemed the lowest common denominator of the uniform basis of the life of all families in every society and the uniform expectation of all families, namely, reproduction of the population, its socialisation within dominant values, the economic and caring functions... Though the economic function has been the cause of argument, no one has thought to look at how differently this function is realised in different social groups, how in each society (including our own) the economic and social interests of one group of families conflict with the interests of other groups, etc. Furthermore, it is only natural that the values by which different groups socialise their children differ.

Up till now, no attention has been paid to the discrete interests and values specific to particular groups, i.e. how individual social groups and developmental types of family differ, and where their existential interests find themselves in mutual conflict. All of the research conducted in this sphere over the past twenty years deals with the "socialist family". Leaving aside a couple of incomplete exceptions, there are no studies analysing a specific group of families and their particular problems, needs and interests, not to speak of the conflict between the interests of families from the highest and lowest rungs of society. Functional analysis "overemphasises the normative element in social life, minimises the importance of social conflict at the expense of social solidarity, stresses the harmonious nature of social systems, and fails to account for social change" (Cohen 1968: 48), to quote from the textbook summary of the critique of the substantive weaknesses of functionalism. The question of why the "residium" of familiarism in this country has clearly grown stronger instead of weakening, as one would expect, is beyond the scope of functionalist analysis, which is based on teleological apriorism.

It is for the reader to decide to what extent this failure of functionalism can be attributed to its ideologically conservative bias.

3.

Albeit in a different context, Ferdinand Mount (1882)[15] pointed out that all ideologies are inherently hostile to the family. They try to interpret and adapt it to their own ends, something the family has always resisted. The family has always relentlessly pursued its own objectives, which are essentially unchanging. This hostility is

---

15 Mount takes issue with the powerful surge of historical sociology of the family beginning in the early 1970s (Ariès, Stone, Mittenauer…). It is beyond the scope of this study to investigate to what extent he is right, especially in his claim regarding the invariability of the family.

especially evident shortly after a revolution, i.e. after a change of the ruling ideology. Each revolution is openly or covertly hostile to the family. It cannot be otherwise, since people find their loyalties split between family and revolutionary movement. The family drains the strength of even the most faithful followers and diverts their attention from the revolutionary struggle, even in those most critical moments when everything is to play for.

Post-revolutionary enthusiasm in this country, too, was by no means favourably inclined toward the family and its small, private world. It launched its appeal to the individual, the man in the crowd, and its concept of collectivism had more of a political orientation (the collectivism of a movement structured mainly by age or sector: the Socialist Youth Movement, work collectives, the trade-union collectivism of factory recreation, etc.). Politically activist materials and engaged works of art evidence this. Films from the early 1950s above all offer a wealth of sociological material in this respect.

However, this was not simply a question of a new rhetoric. For the Marxist revolution the decisive lever of change was the economy. The new regime expropriated the family, fully cognisant of what it was doing. It stripped it of its economic subjectivity and sovereignty by proclaiming the family business or enterprise to be illegal. In some cases (e.g. repair services) this was done at the expense of economic rationality. But this was how things had to be: the revolution demanded it. In order to consolidate its hold on power it was necessary to break the solid structure of family networks and to place itself at the head of a population homogenised by the uniform status of employee.

The first stage of the family's adaptation to this new situation was assimilation. The family accommodated itself to the reality of the new socialist state to which it had to conform, unless its individual members had already fully identified themselves with the aims of the movement. In return for placing strict limits on the expansion of family assets, the new societal organisation offered or promised the family considerable advantages. Women could now be liberated from never-ending household drudgery and enjoy a new dignity based on economic independence in paid employment. In addition, they were promised a "liberated household" within the imminent future of the socialist system of services. Tradesmen and small business owners as heads of families were offered the unprecedented security of fixed employment and relief from the pressure of competition. Farm workers now enjoyed regular working hours and, in time, even Saturday off, while many labourers were recruited into the expanding bureaucracy and offered cleaner work. Young people were appointed to comfortable jobs and appreciated the firm promise of an apartment within a fair system of allocation without investment and worries, cheap workers' canteens, and day-care centres and nurseries free of charge. Instead of religion and its promise of an eternal life in heaven, people were offered social justice in the here and now. They were assured that the country would outstrip capitalism by the end of the sixties and that "this current generation would live to see communism", etc.

Of course, not everyone believed in all the promises, nor was everyone equally enthused by the new values. However, the psychology behind the advantages on offer appealed to young people especially, with their natural sense for collectivism, egalitarianism and optimism. The instrumental concept of the family in relation to a higher-order collectivism was not too much of an obstacle for young families, and offered the illusion of a extended youth. Young families founded in the fifties adopted the new ideology without any great problem, even if they were not whole-hearted adherents. Along with Mount one could say that the new ideology successfully reinterpreted the family and among young people appropriated it to its own ends, or at least obliged people to accept it as essentially the most pragmatic solution.

This victory was firmly based on economic reality and power. However, ideologically it was frail. After all, it is not difficult to coerce a family into surrendering its previous selfishness: it is considerably more difficult, however, to persuade it that this is for the best. This was the task of the entire system of political education, the mass media, schools and science. Like the functionalist theory of family, public rhetoric attempted to persuade everyone that the family occupied many irreplaceable social functions, the fulfilment of which could be deemed a "task", and that people who did not measure up to this task were egoistic parasites doing harm to society. The instrumental concept of family was more tangible beneath the surface of activism and propaganda than in sociological theory.

However, science has no monopoly on social theory. Everyone has their own social theory. Everyone can explain their own destiny, their social status, and the function of individual institutions, and everyone can hazard a guess at the interests hidden behind the obstacles that impede the fulfilment of their natural needs and wants. Furthermore, everyone tries to take in not only the social world around them, but also the nature, origin and purpose of the explanations they receive of this world. They would like to know who exactly is offering the explanation and why it is this and not some other explanation. People differ in such matters. However, in general one can say that Czechs appear to display a high level of vigilance and caution: they are, one might say, something of a distrustful people.

It is no wonder that the Czechs sensed the sleight of hand, the catch involved in the instrumental concept of the family. While academics and the media loftily explained the functions of the family within the socialist state, the families in question were increasingly inclined to ask: "But what purpose does the state serve our family?"

For the plain fact is that certain promises were never fulfilled. There is no point in enumerating them. Even the most theoretically minded are aware of the shortage of flats and household services, the failures of medical care and education, and other family demands traditionally met by the state. Not only did a rural teacher have to build a house with his own hands, but he also had to lay a drainpipe and connect it to the public sewage system, or in some cases he and his neighbours had to create an entire sewage system. Families had not only to reconcile themselves to their children having to learn in overcrowded classrooms, sometimes even on shifts, but also discovered to their surprise that the state was unable to provide a school education without the help of those same parents. A child whose parents could not explain to them at home what the teacher was unable to manage in the packed classroom was simply out of luck. As for higher education, it was selective, highly selective...

However, the families did not complain. There was no one to complain to, in any case. They took matters into their own hands, as they had always done since time immemorial. After a short period of groping around in the dark, families rapidly revitalised traditional kinship networks, a non-monetary exchange of goods and services, and achieved an unprecedented level of self-sufficiency. The benefits flowing from this second economy increasingly began to determine the status and prospects of a family.

The basic problem that families had to solve in this regard was their stunted economic independence. The illegality of family businesses imposed strict limits on family entrepreneurship in the broadest sense of the word, not to mention economic expansion and growth. Surpluses could be accumulated by the skilful utilisation of family resources or by pursuing an intelligent strategy to ensure advantageous positions and a rise in the status of individual family members. These surpluses could not, however, be used for investment purposes. In fact, everything had to be consumed on the spot. While in the West, consumer society is being hotly debated, one way or another the Czechs silently realised it.

However, it gradually became clear that even this obstacle could be surmounted. Though a conveniently located petrol station is difficult to purchase, securing a job as manager for your nephew was possible with a little judicious outlay (what an independent observer would call a bribe). The same was true of the Mototechna second-hand car dealership, a butcher's shop, the pub on the square, and many other places it would be too dangerous to mention. The entire official network of goods and services could be viewed as the economic basis for the autonomy of the families doing business in it. In addition to the profit made or loss incurred by the state, family profits were to be made by providing a reciprocal service, e.g. moving someone up a waiting list, getting one's hands on goods that were otherwise practically unavailable... These were non-monetary profits. However, there were also monetary profits to be made, from overpricing goods, cheating, theft, bribery... In its way, this was an ideal arrangement, and one that made a lot of families happy, not only those who did business in this way (from the winemakers of south Moravia to the waiters of Krkonoše),[16] but also those who profited from their enterprise: offered protection, rubberstamped people nominated for official positions, helped smooth over legal problems... The families creamed off the profit while the state shelled out on expenses. And incurred the losses. And got poorer. The state covered the cost of heating, electricity and rent, while the families did business and become wealthy.

All of this resulted in the redefinition of the concept of ownership as understood by the man in the street. As Leonid Abalkin, an academic and the director of the Economic Institute of the Soviet Academy of Sciences, points out, at first sight things in socialist ownership appear to be the common property of everyone, and at second sight the property of no one. In fact, from an economic point of view, they are the property of those who have the right of disposal. This in turn establishes ownership, albeit illegitimate and not subject to oversight (Abalkin 1989). This right can even become a market value or commodity. Whatever the case, it is a social reality and

---

16 I leave Slovakia to one side. This entire essay, based on personal observation, is an attempt to arrive at a better understanding of the Bohemian lands. How much of what I write applies to Slovakia is a question for my readers to answer based on their judgement and experience. In 1987, when I wrote this text, I was already convinced that Slovakia was a different kind of society.

a far more reliable base than social rhetoric, which describes things differently.

The family arrived at a reinterpretation of socialist ownership and, in a broader sense, the relationship between private and state ownership, far more quickly than researchers at the Academy of Sciences. It offered its courteous thanks for the post-revolutionary interpretation of the function of the state and family, before proceeding to create its own explanation of social reality on different principles. Should we wish to look for parallels between the layman's interpretation of social reality and that of theoretical discourse, then we might say that functionalist analysis receded into the background to be replaced by another school of interpretation. Paradoxical as it may seem, this new school of popular thought – with which our sociology took such issue, accusing it of the deadly sin of being petit bourgeois and declaring it a hangover from the past – is very close to classical Marxism in terms of its basic explicatory principle.

Its basic category of interpretation is not that of function, but of interest: a supra-individual, group interest. In addition, there are two other similarities pointing to the homology of the structures of the intellectual world of classical Marxism and the popular interpretation of the lived experience of our social reality: conflict of interest as the driving force of social life; and the criterion of practice as the last instance of the legitimacy of theory.

It soon came to the attention of the average Czech family that those who rejected the official reinterpretation of the family and retained familiarism as their worldview were socially far more successful than those families that, in all good faith, took to their breasts an instrumental understanding of the family in respect of the social reality of a higher order. A family oriented on a familiaristic theoretical interpretation was quite successful in promoting its interests even under extremely vexatious conditions. To begin with the state was successful in its reinterpretation of the family and in the subjugation of the sources of its economic sources and power, and thus to an extent in its attempt to create a new-order collectivism. However, things did not remain that way for long. The result was not easily discernible at first, though these days is impossible to overlook: the family eventually colonised the state.

These days, the average Czech family deliberately focuses the energies of all its members on the promotion and defence of its interests. It knows that these interests are realised at the intersection of the conflicting interests of other families. It also knows that the nuclear family as an isolated unit is at a disadvantage and will find it difficult to survive unless it joins forces with other nuclear families, preferably on the basis of kinship networks that constitute the modern analogue of the traditional family. The average Czech family also knows that individual family clans must form higher-order coalitions between themselves, and that what in theoretical discourse might be called "class instinct" orientates them when determining which interests of other families are in conflict with their own interests.

Familiarism has become a very influential philosophy of the lived world, and thus an important social force. In the end it has reinterpreted even the state, to the extent of perceiving positions in the state apparat as familial resources. In its extreme form it sets loyalty to the family in opposition to loyalty to higher units, with the result that, even in the case of traditional moral standards, complete disloyalty to non-family interests is in the interest of the family: *He who does not rob the state, robs his own family*.

Of course, not all families are equally successful in this world of social conflict and sharp-elbowed competition between family clans. Another snag in the functional interpretation of the family can be expressed as follows: who precisely is this state?

However, though second in line, this question is far from being subordinate. On the contrary, in terms of understanding the perspective of lived experience it is crucial. By asking it, the ordinary person defines for themselves the problem of why they are being offered an instrumentally functional explanation of the family, and why their own theory of conflicting family interests remains unformulated by social rhetoric. It would seem that the social space is not as opaque for the "non-theorist" as it is for the theorist. Many a theoretician is a greater victim of the mystification from which they make a living than those for whom such mystification is intended.[17]

Should a real-world reader observe who is offering them the instrumental interpretation and how they are behaving, the answer within the familiarist conception of society will be very consistent: they are simply other families. In a smaller community in which people know each other from their early school years and the local "aristocracy" is within reach socially, the extended family networks linking centres of local government, economic life and political power cannot remain invisible. And if anyone speaks of the "needs of society" being superior to the petit-bourgeois selfishness of families, while at the same time happening to belong to these networks, then popular theory has no problem interpreting his motives.

* * *

Not much needs to be added to this three-year-old text to make the inertia of Czech society during the 1970s and 1980s comprehensible. However, we must not allow ourselves to be seduced by a more superficial observation, expressed in another popular saying, namely,

---

17 That the situation was not as obscure for the ordinary person as it might appear to the uninitiated after studying the economic literature of that time is encapsulated in a joke that I would like to record here for future historians. I first heard it in Moscow, where it was called *Chetyre chudiesa socializma* (Four Miracles of Socialism). It was especially popular in Czechoslovakia in the 1970s. The Czechs took great pleasure in the word *chudiesa* (miracle), though increased the number to six. So here we go: First miracle: There's no unemployment, though nobody actually works. Second miracle: Nobody works, but everyone gets paid. Third miracle: Everyone gets paid, but there's nothing to buy with the money. Fourth miracle: No one can buy anything, but everyone owns everything. (Then came the Czech contribution.) Fifth miracle: Everyone owns everything, but no one is satisfied. Sixth miracle: No one is satisfied, but 99% of the people vote for the system. During the 1970s and 1980s I knew no better way of explaining the situation in this country to foreign visitors than by recounting this joke.

"They pretend to pay us and we pretend to work", and then explain the persistence of the situation as the outcome of what, in the end, was a reasonably satisfactory "social contract". For sure there was a degree of balance and something like a tacit arrangement. But it had been dysfunctional arrangement for years before it came to an end.

It was dysfunctional, but it lasted. The basic problem for ordinary people was the lack of a positive alternative. People lacked a model of behaviour that was more dignified and productive than that which families themselves had developed in the process of adapting to the reality of socialism. The colonisation of the state was a huge success under difficult conditions. But in the end everyone could see that this would lead to a complete collapse during which no one would be spared. Yet no other acceptable model was on the table.

The dissidents? Let's not kid ourselves: *the dissidents, too, were simply "other families"*,[18] and for those possessed of good old-fashioned common sense, not particularly trustworthy families at that. Indeed, when someone with a nose for class differences discerned a division into two irreconcilable classes, namely those at the top and those at the bottom, and then attempted to classify dissident groups within this structure, they were at best somewhat discomfited. And were they to inquire further into what it was exactly that united dissident circles into a classifiable clan, they would recognise some inauspicious signs.

To begin with, they would notice that dissident families included many of those who had participated in the demolition of their own traditional world in the early 1950s. The pieces having been put back

---

18 Here and throughout the text I use the word "family" in its broadest and even figurative sense. I have shown elsewhere [Možný 1982] that the overwhelming majority of the population does not live in an autonomous "nuclear family". Under the surface, our society is structured in networks reminiscent of the classical "extended family". Even today they are not far from the traditional form of "networks of blood and power", interconnected, overlapping, and hierarchised within clientelism.

together again after a fashion, they would then see these same families, in a new experiment plainly motivated by a guilty conscience, once more take a hammer to the everyday existence of ordinary people in 1968, this time in the name of those selfsame "correct" ideals that had already failed once. In the world of common sense, practice is a ruthless criterion of truth, and high ideals that come apart upon the slightest encounter with reality can no longer serve as lodestar for a reasonable person.

Back in the mid-1960s, when explaining why he had joined the communist movement, Ludvík Vaculík observed that, right from the start, the movement included "ill-informed idealists". The only criticism I have of this description is that the adjective is redundant: for those possessed of sound judgement, "ill-informed" is the very definition of an idealist. The description is a tautology, to which one might simply add that being ignorant is a critical component of the idealist's armoury. Which in turn led to a second suspicion that diminished the credit of the dissidents, namely, whether a certain idealism (i.e. ignorance) was not in fact an innate characteristic of these circles.

It was not that common sense deemed the dissidents to be stupid. Good heavens, no! The ordinary person respected their intelligence and recognised that they were far more informed than they. However, it was the relevance of this knowledge to the fragile quotidian world that gave pause for thought. Long before Thomas Kuhn and Karl Mannheim, common sense had perceived the multi-paradigmatic nature of an acquaintance with the social universe and its connection to social inclusion. Of course, just as one will find scientists who are genuinely convinced that science is the only reliable key to an adequate understanding of reality, and that all other belief systems are merely its precursors or simply various types of naivety, so even among those who have not received a training in scientific thinking there are many who consider their own way of thinking to be the only correct, if not the only possible, way of thinking.

In general, ordinary families recognised that the dissidents had a right to their truth: they were simply unsure as to whether this was a truth they shared or even wished to share. They respected the opinions of dissidents and saw the value of this alternative way of thinking (and living) for a healthy social organism. Long before academic sociology concluded, after much discussion in the 1970s, that the parallel existence of multiple paradigms did not discredit it in the scientific world, but in fact enriched it (anyone interested in this should read the original essay by Petrusek, 1986), popular social theory knew why the world contained weirdoes, prophets and eccentrics, and why there were large groups of people in society who thought differently to most others: who, to pluck an example at random, "lived in truth". However, the conclusion that "we cannot all be dissidents" followed on logically from this wisdom too, and played its part in maintaining the oppressive immobility of the past twenty years.

The lamentation that "we cannot all be dissidents..." incorporated within it a vertical dimension containing three implications. Firstly, there was recognition of the moral superiority of dissident circles and a humble acknowledgement on the part of the ordinary person that this was something they lacked: that they were not courageous enough, that they were too inclined to yield to the siren song of consumption, fine things and a comfortable life, that the age-old weakness of the body was also their master, that they feared for their young and the hard-won nest they had created for them...

And then there was another difference, not quite vertical, more a variation on Havel's immortal image of a greengrocer who places a sign in his shop window with the words *Workers of the world unite!* in order to demonstrate his loyalty to the regime and thus protect his small world. We see the same ritualistic gesture in the conduct – and here I will choose as a representative a similarly extreme type – of a neurosurgeon who swots up on the ludicrous idea of the laws of the socialist economy and the sheer nonsense of a counter-revolutionary conspiracy in the 1960s, in order to parrot them during an examination at the Večerní univerzita marxismu-leninismu (Evening University of Marxism-Leninism – VUML). He may not have read Havel (or, on the contrary, has got his hands on a samizdat edition and knows him well), but he knows that what he is doing represents a humiliating gesture of loyalty to a criminal regime for which he has only deep contempt, and that he undergoes this degrading ritual in order to save his own small world. But if he had refused to make this gesture, it would not only have meant losing a well paid job (in which he often works sixty hours a week, night shifts and weekends, but which he nevertheless loves). In itself that wouldn't mean much. At most he would have ended up as a general practitioner in a small clinic (and if this were in South Moravia, I happen to know for a fact, as does our brain surgeon, that he would work half the hours for twice the pay, albeit not in the form of a salary [but in the form of kickbacks: t/n]). However, it also meant his patients losing his competence, a reflection not only of his special talent, but the years of toil at the operating table, the toil from which he might otherwise have built a little monument to himself. And our surgeon feels that his talent and this monument are not his and his alone. He feels that he must flex his moral spine in order to continue using his scalpel to put other spines to rights, regardless of the morality of their owners, since this is where his talent and primary responsibility lie.

The fact that the proportion of doctors as opposed to writers among the signatories of Charter 77 is an exact inversion of their representation in the population at large has yet to be explained. Any consideration of the dissidents is pointless here, since they have put this debate behind them, having had it sometime in 1979.[19]

---

19 The debate was prompted by an essay by Petr Pithart entitled *Pokus o vlast* (Attempt at a Homeland, 1979). The entire debate is summarised well in Pithart's book *Dějiny a politika* (History and Politics, 1990).

However, in place of my surgeon, Vaculík drew on a far more tasteful prototype: the ordinary baker. It complicates matters, as even Havel knows, that most Gypsies do not live entirely in truth, and yet in their own inalienable way they are for him decent people, and discussions on this topic still await us. The specialist language for this discussion is offered to us by no less than Peter Berger in his essay *Moral Considerations and Political Action* (published in Czech in 1990). Berger distinguishes between the morality of truth and the morality of responsibility, and points to the fact that these two reference points for moral conduct may not always overlap. Keeping them apart was one of the devilish tricks played by the old regime, and ignoring this fact means descending, even on the level of specialist discourse, into mutual accusations of treachery.

However, let us return to the problem of why the vast majority of the population perceived the dissidents as "different families", and how they classified them in their social universe. In addition to the vertical dimension of acknowledged superiority, and alongside this awareness of respected functional difference, there was a third, downward oriented, vertical perception. In an upside-down social world, this meant that even dissident circles were perceived as comprising merely a special kind of "aristocratic" family. In terms of folk wisdom, after all, these were people who, like the communists, "lived off ideas", and whose status was embedded in a world of public respect. Their notoriety, even if negative, afforded them privileges that the ordinary person did not enjoy,[20] and this was the fly in the ointment of their moral integrity. They paid a high price for such integrity, to be sure, but at the same time inadvertently and perversely it also paid off handsomely for them.

---

20 Sometime in the early eighties, a mildly intoxicated, regional police commissioner and amateur student of sociology confided in me the following: "These days, if you really want to be treated in accordance with the law, you either have to be in the nomenklatura [a list of names drawn up by the Communist Party from which candidates were selected for senior positions in the government apparat: t/n], or a well known dissident. Your average Joe has no such rights, Dr Možný."

However, given their intelligence, dissident circles sensed this fly in the ointment of their own status from the first moment they were marginalised by the ruling power and denigrated at every opportunity. They defended themselves with all the means available to them. The threat posed to the regime by the Výbor pro ochranu nespravedlivě stíhaných (Committee for the Defence of the Unjustly Prosecuted) resided in the fact that it deliberately shattered the exclusive status of known dissidents and drew attention to the less well known. The state security service hated this committee more than it did Charter 77, and was well aware of the reason. In this respect not even the sternest moral critic can fault our dissidents.

However, not even the most altruistic endeavour to renounce all advantages could eradicate one element of exclusivity. It could not, even had it wanted to, which it did not. This was the exclusivity based on the far greater *social and cultural capital* of dissident circles, a capital of which the ordinary person could only dream. I use these terms as they are used by Bourdieu (1977), and they will serve me below with greater significance. But for the moment, let us use them descriptively. The important structures of the dissident circles were created by "men of letters", scholars, people from the world of the written word. Those of the workers who joined them tended to be well read autodidacts, people of cultivated tastes. Many came to the movement via their religious faith, unconventionally experienced as a call for active participation in the whole of the European spiritual and cultural legacy: others through an innate curiosity of a decidedly secular nature. The critical thinking that pitted them against the regime and led them to a life in truth also meant they read extensively. Even their cultural capital significantly outstripped that of an averagely educated civil servant, not to speak of people without a secondary school education. In theory everyone could acquire such capital. In practice, however, it was not quite that simple and most people did not possess it.

Understandably, the ordinary person on the street was not familiar with Habermas's theory of the increasing importance of "communicative competence". Similarly, they would not have been up to speed with the theories of Nisbet, Collins and others, who claim that communication skills now define a new ruling class.[21] This class avails itself of its exclusive ability to master the information explosion and the instant electronic connectivity of the modern world that now forms the basis of its social and physical reproduction, in order to establish and exert a new kind of dominion. Nevertheless, the ordinary working person instinctively divined that, by virtue of their cultural capital, the dissident circles already latently belonged amongst their betters, and in light of the experience they had already had with their nomenclatural betters, it is no wonder that they kept their distance.

And we have not yet even begun a comparison of social capital. For here, too, there was such a chasm between the ordinary person and dissident circles that it took extraordinary courage – or naivety – to bridge it. *Don't venture onto the ice with the lords, Vašek...*[22] When an ordinary Czech family compared the flimsiness of its own clan's social network, skilled at accessing substandard goods but vulnerable to the creepy touch of power, with that of the dissidents, it grasped immediately that the path trodden by the latter was not a realistic option. The dissidents had contacts beyond the border of the municipality, which is where the power of ordinary clans generally ended. The dissidents had contacts outside the very republic. Not only in Bratislava, which was surprising enough in itself, but also in Paris, London, Uppsala, New York... The ordinary

21　It is worth noting that when I use the term "new class", I am not referring to the concept discussed by Djilas (1957), but to the meaning the term has in the texts referred to by Habermas, Collins and Nisbet (and most explicitly in the work of Gouldner 1979), i.e. I am not implying *a priori* evaluative or political connotations, but using the word purely as an analytical term.
22　From an epigram by Karel Havlíček Borovský that continues: "*... for we know of many an example of the master slipping and the peasant breaking his leg on his behalf.*" t/n.

person heard a clear signal: *Don't venture onto the ice with the lords, Vašek...*

In addition to the unambiguous advantages enjoyed by dissident circles in terms of cultural, and consequently, social capital, a discreet question mark also hung over their more worldly assets. Envy is a human trait that sociology cannot overlook, and the class instinct is unusually sensitive to differences in material well-being. Kohout's beautiful apartment, a Renault from TUZEX[23], a villa near the Sázava river, Havel's legendary millions, and the orgies organised by Vaculík using dollars from espionage centres... this was the image of Czech dissidence created and propagated by the regime.

On a conscious level, ordinary folk on the whole rejected these images. However, probe more deeply and a different story emerges. Even random encounters with well known dissidents reinforced at least some of the suspicions harboured by ordinary folk. When a plumber, even a wealthy moonlighter enjoying plentiful kickbacks, entered the home of an opponent of the regime and compared it to his own, he could not help but see the difference. His own apartment was undoubtedly more lavishly furnished, while this one was kind of threadbare. However, the objects in his own apartment were only pale imitations of the genuine article to be found in this apartment. Everything here was authentic, a difference that we do not perceive until things are laid next to each other, but which we then immediately identify as crucial. This is why the nouveau riche will never believe that old money, however down-at-heel, is genuinely poorer off.

However, understanding the character of the difference between "old" and "new" wealth was impossible. The regime took advantage of the "total occupation of the public semantic space" (Ash 1990) and did not allow for open debate regarding the issues we have touched

---

23 A network of state-run shops that did not accept Czechoslovak currency but only vouchers purchased using foreign currency. These shops supplied luxury items, local goods in short supply, and foreign goods: t/n.

upon here. Even on the side of the dissidents, there were internal restrictions placed on critical self-reflection under the conditions of an irreconcilable struggle to the death. (I, too, in the version of this essay submitted for publication in the spring of 1989, sought to avoid these problems for reasons that must be obvious.) Whatever one's implacable will to truth, strategic considerations existed. Opening up for inspection the genuine social status of dissident families was not possible, and the gut instinct that the general population was forced to fall back on advised it not to trust anyone whatsoever.[24]

Bringing together all of these facts, we find ourselves in agreement with Pareto that the dissident movement represented a counter-elite with a relatively narrow and unclear social base. As regards elementary questions of group interests, its aims were not clearly articulated. The "relevance structure" of its aims did not satisfactorily correspond to the relevance structure of lived experience. The dissidents were brought together by a negative programme involving rejection of the existing order and by a basic concept of civil society. Quite how this society would react to the fact of social and economic inequality was a question left open for discussion when, if ever, it became pertinent.

However, even the dissidents faced one unpleasant question posed by the people, to which they had no clear answer: *That's all very well. But what about the property?*

To someone fighting for the basic human rights of this very population, the question might appear distasteful, unworthy of their attention. However, that was a luxury they could afford. And if, on the contrary, they took the question seriously, they soon found that the members of their circle were divided as to the answer and that,

---

24 Petrusek (1989: 212) explains the rational basis of this mistrust very well: "To put things very simply: those who have cultural capital also have the ability to demonstrate their legitimacy, the legitimacy of their social position and above all the legitimacy of their symbolic dominance and authority by means of a range of resources that those with 'only' human capital do not have at their disposal."

under the circumstances, they could not afford to articulate these differences without this jeopardising the far more important goal of overthrowing the conditions that had prevented the creation of public discourse and the constitution of a normal political space. And this is not to speak of the internal discord within dissident circles themselves.

This offers a satisfactory explanation of the status and strategy of dissident circles, and also helps explain why the general population wavered for so long before finally joining forces with the dissidents.

Chapter Two

How could it have happened so smoothly?

In light of the above, it might seem that answering the second of our questions – *how was it that the old regime ended up collapsing so fast?* – will prove difficult.

We may have to switch the frame of reference and adopt the perspective of historian or political scientist, who will state the reasons for the inevitable collapse of the entire system of post-totalitarian society in Czechoslovakia with confidence. Let's take a moment to remind ourselves of events.

First of all, there was the collapse of Soviet power, which had provided external support for a regime with zero legitimacy.

(A sociologist would merely add that the legitimacy of power had from the very start, i.e. from the Russian invasion in 1968, not been quite zero. Like other conquered populations, ours granted a form of entitlement, albeit bespoiled, to the government of collaborationists. Can a nation on its knees afford to be choosy? At least to begin with it was expected that Husák[25] and his henchmen would serve the nation as stewards of the national interest during a period of defeat. The pragmatically minded realised that Husák would have to reach serious compromises with the occupying power, and the realistically minded understood that he would use this opportunity to pursue his own personal interests. However, as long as he did not venture beyond a certain limit, he would also fulfil a certain historical mission. In other words, someone had to do the dirty work, and if that someone was to be Husák, then he deserved a modicum of recognition, albeit coupled with disdain, since you only have to perform such work once and your claim to honour and dignity is flushed down the pan. However, he contributed something to his community. And so Husák and his like enjoyed a degree of legitimacy. However, even this was gradually lost, and with the arrival of Gorbachev on the scene it disappeared without trace.

---

25 First Secretary of the Communist Party of Czechoslovakia from 1969 to 1987 and president of Czechoslovakia from 1975 to 1989, i.e. a near perfect overlap with normalisation: t/n.

The Russian Bear now faced so many problems of its own that the feverish endeavour of the collaborationists to divert its attention was no longer needed.)

In addition to the collapse of Soviet support, whether through the direct exertion of power or the indirect legitimising strategies referred to above, other factors will no doubt be brought to our attention and analysed. There was the influence of the impressive social and political developments taking place in Poland and Hungary. And one cannot overlook the irresistibly demonstrative flight of people from East Germany into the warm embrace of capitalism, followed from the windows of apartments in Prague's Malá Strana[26] (and indeed, the arrogance with which the fleeing Germans left their Trabants in the hands of Czechs was intolerable)[27]. Historians will no doubt point to the woeful miscalculations of pretenders to the throne, successors to the now written-off political generation of consolidators, which sowed the seeds of their own destruction. Economists will find answers in the desperate economic plight the country found itself in, lacking a wedge with which to knock out the old wedge[28]. The general consensus was that no "package of measures" would help this time round, since this involved the breakdown of macroeconomic relations... Is there anything left for the humble sociologist, rummaging around in this bundle of explanations? And if so, is there room for a sociologist of the family with their special micro-perspective? Do we have anything whatsoever to offer without leaving our family yard?

---

26   The Lesser Quarter, where a number of embassies are situated, including that of Western Germany, whither the East Germans fled: t/n.
27   The East Germans crossed over into Czechoslovakia in Trabants, which they then left in Prague upon entering the West German embassy: t/n).
28   From the Czech proverb *vytloukat klín klínem* meaning to knock out a wedge that has got stuck in wood with another wedge, and variously translated as "fight fire with fire", "like cures like", more temptingly as "take a hair of the dog", or, somewhat less correctly, albeit accurately, "forget a woman with another woman": t/n.

Though the pickings will be slim, let's pick away. There is no one key that opens the door to understanding history. We will always be obliged to explore wider contexts, since the forces that drive family trees have not only deep roots, but a variegated crown of macro-social contexts. We have no reason to avoid the macro, but let us for the moment return patiently to the micro-perspective.

The simple answer to the question of why the old regime collapsed so smoothly is that, in the end, it did not meet anyone's needs. It did not meet the opposition's needs, and it did not even meet the needs of those they were opposing. Not only did it not meet the needs of those at the bottom: it didn't meet the needs of those at the top either. Especially those at the top, paradoxically.

The explanation will at first sight appear to be economic in nature. We can indeed accept it as an economic explanation as long as we think in terms of the political economy, or even better, if we understand the term "economy" as sociologists use it in analytical practice [e.g. the political economy, the economy of power, etc.: t/n]. It is crucial that we do not fall into the trap of defining economics too narrowly, as tends to be the case when the talk is of "economic reform".

For a sociologist, assets represent merely one of the guises that power takes. This is nothing new. Plato saw three legitimate sources of power in the state: the rich, soldiers, and philosophers; in other words, money, weapons and knowledge. Modern sociology simply emphasises the convertibility of these three forms of power and adds others where appropriate. As far back as the late 1930s, Bertrand Russell attempted to introduce an approach into the practice of sociology that would draw on a concept of power as the supreme explicatory principle and understand it as the highest common denominator of all social affairs, in much the same way as energy is understood by modern physics. He writes:

"Like energy, power has many forms, such as wealth, armaments, civil authority, influence on opinion. No one of these can be regarded as subordinate to any other, and there is no one form from which the others are derivative. The attempt to treat one form of power, say wealth, in isolation, can only be partially successful, just as the study of one form of energy will be defective at certain points, unless other forms are taken into account. Wealth may result from military power or from influence over opinion, just as either of these may result from wealth." (Russell 1938)[29]

Among those who have attempted to enlarge on the three basic forms of power, Pierre Bourdieu has a huge influence today. When interpreting the difference in the status of the families of dissidents and ordinary people, I drew on two terms, undefined and thus far intuitively grasped, which Bourdieu successfully introduced into sociology in order to explain other forms of power (or wealth or influence). These are the terms *cultural capital* and *social capital*, which to begin with were closely intertwined (cf. Bourdieu 1977), though subsequently became analytically distinguishable forms of power, notwithstanding a continuing degree of overlap.

For the sake of orientation, and at the risk of over-simplification, we can say that the source of cultural capital is a certain ability (skill, power, potency) to handle information, especially information that forms the content of symbols. As I will show below, such skill can be accumulated and saved for a rainy day, i.e. it can be converted into capital that pays out interest without losing its value.

29 Russell's initiative did not meet with a direct response from sociology, both because it came from a philosopher and it came at the wrong time… However, the problem of power is a permanent albeit implicit feature of sociological literature, and different trends simply conceptualised it in different ways, and when analysing it shifted the emphasis between its various forms. During the 1960s, a revived interest in a Marxist view of society focused attention on the problem of political and economic power and contributed to the development of conflict theory (albeit with a significant contribution from non-Marxist approaches that responded with their own interpretation of conflict – cf. Keller 1990). The most recent to respond directly to Russell's initiative is Runciman 1989.

Social capital, on the other hand, is based on an ability to create complex social networks, to understand how these networks intersect, and to use this knowledge to one's own benefit, especially by manoeuvring oneself and one's loved ones into the most strategically advantageous positions. This skill can also be accumulated, as I will show below.

All of us have a degree of cultural and social capital, just as everyone has some money, wisdom and, without question, power. *The little people are generally afraid of the big people, but the biggest people are most afraid of the little people,* as the popular comedian Jan Werich observes.

1.

Let us for the time being stick with the wisdom of the "little people". In the first part of this essay we decided this referred to the social construction of reality as performed by common sense in the face of the ideologisation being practised by the "big people". So let us look at the situation from their perspective. Only then, when we have cleared the table and created some order, will we attempt to answer the difficult but crucially important question of what it was about the old arrangement that did not suit the families of the ruling establishment.

So first off: what was *not* to the advantage of an ordinary Czech family? What led to its growing dissatisfaction, dissatisfaction, even though it was playing its part in the successful colonisation of the state? The answer, strange to say, was not the division of the social world that we described as an almost class-based antagonistic division of society into us and them, the former at the bottom, the latter on the top. A basic feature of common sense is that it does not attempt to resist the realities of the lived world, but accepts them realistically as an almost natural state of affairs and focuses on adaptation rather than confrontation.

The reality of the social vertical is one such fact. An ordinary person knows that there always has been and always will be an elite. There is nothing to be done about it. What is permitted to some is withheld from others. That's just how the world works. José Ortega y Gasset is right, of course, to point to the "revolt of the masses" and the sheer impertinence of the ordinary man of our modern times, who has lost an awareness of his own limits and goes around shoving his snout into any trough he can find. However, Ortega y Gasset also points out that it took more than three centuries before ordinary people began to believe Enlightenment ideas regarding the legitimacy of aspirations for social equality, and Adorno adds that it takes the ongoing, everyday efforts of the venal power of all media to sustain this awareness.

Even so, there remains a kind of ambivalence, a state in which a person simultaneously believes that they are equal to the next person and has the same rights as everyone else, while at the same time sensing that this is not true. The signals that ordinary people received from the old regime reinforced this ambivalence, since the rhetoric spoke of equality, while the practice consisted of the selective distribution of privileges.

But if it was not inequality that offended the poorer off, then what was it? At first glance, the answer may appear both trivial and, in the narrowest sense of the word, economic. An inability to look more deeply also led to well known packages of (economic) measures, not even the periodic failure of which helped their creators to grasp their error of their ways.

So what was actually going on?

The macroeconomic problems of the socialist state were manifest on the microeconomic level of the finances of ordinary Czech families by virtue of the slow decline of the market over the long-term. An economist would say there was more money than goods. To which a young wife might reply: I'm having more and more difficulty getting by to the end of the month. Both were right and both missed the point. In reality, the growing problem was that money was no longer the main problem (though, of course, everyone found themselves out of pocket from time to time), either for the "large economy", which for years had operated on the "soft budget constraint" principle (Kornai 1981), or for the small consumer, who, notwithstanding the money in her hand, found it increasingly difficult to actually find what it was she wanted, and needed, to spend it on.

Three levels of distribution were created.

Even before goods arrived in the distribution network, members of the nomenklatura and apparat had first right of refusal and selected the most sought after items from local warehouses after greasing the palm of the producer and/or the importer. Getting one's hands on certain goods simply meant being on personal terms with the official overseeing trade or industry on the level of the Regional Committee of the Communist Party or higher. Some goods were so precious that they were earmarked for said official and his immediate family, the result being that not even he had access to a surplus with which he might continue trading.

What was left over from this first market (which in fairness tended to be a fair amount in the case of most goods) then entered the shops. However, here, too, these goods did not immediately reach the shelves, but found themselves circulating on the second-order market. The workers of distribution chains took their pick of what was on offer before the shop opened. And there were many such workers, from the apparatchiks of the central offices, warehouses and interim storage facilities and their families, all the way down to the army of shop assistants and *their* families. In addition, all of these also engaged in a lively trade with the surpluses they managed to get their hands on, exchanging goods amongst themselves and thus craftily dispossessing the nominal shop owner, i.e. the state, in the manner I described in the original essay.

Now, finally, what remained and could not be traded on the second market hit the shelves and was sold over the counter, in such a way that a third market was created. This was the only market that existed officially and was visible from outside, the only market where the customer did not care who the shop assistant was and the shop assistant who the customer was: the only market on which money was the sole currency.

However, supplies to this third market were slowly drying up. Let there be no mistake: this was not caused solely, nor even primarily, by a drop in output. Production plans were met and factories churned out goods, though the lack of transparency of the distribution process meant that these were often goods that no one needed or wanted. However, even these goods fulfilled their function, since they slipped easily through the pre-selection process, created an impression on shop shelves, and thus helped camouflage the existence of the other two higher-order markets. Shops in Czechoslovakia were by no means empty, and a stranger might even form the wrong impression, especially if they had no particular need to buy anything.

The growing dissatisfaction among the population at large was not, therefore, caused by there being no merchandise to buy, but rather by the fact that there was a range of desirable goods that existed on a certain market level, but that could not be obtained by money. A question arose: were these goods that could not be bought for money still "merchandise" in the strict sense, given that the very definition of the word is "that which can be bought for money"?

Families began to look to the future with trepidation, when buying a sack of potatoes would require connections, and when perhaps even bread would be found on the second, or, heaven forfend, the first market, entirely inaccessible to any mere mortal.

And once again the question arose: can we really speak of a market if no money exchanges hands?

And here we bid a definitive farewell to a certain way of thinking that draws an uncompromising line between a planned economy and a market or capitalist economy. And not only are we leaving the discipline of socialist political economy as taught at the Evening

University of Marxism-Leninism (VUML), but also the narrow discipline of economics as a whole. And for good.

For – let us shout it from the rooftops more loudly than a scholarly analysis might permit – let us be in no doubt: *what is taking place before our very eyes at present is not the creation of a market-based society or even a society of market relations. We have always been and will continue to be such a society. From the perspective of social analysis in the strictest sense of the word no society other than a market society exists. Instead, societies appear from time to time that refuse to accept the fact.*

Looked at from this angle, the problem for the ordinary person was as follows: i) the value or power of money was disappearing before their very eyes; ii) social capital was playing an increasingly important role in every transaction; and iii) this way of doing business was becoming more and more costly in terms of time and energy. The situation on the market was becoming difficult to understand, acquiring and maintaining oversight was becoming harder, security was disappearing at a rate of knots, and those families with very limited resources (both material and social) were at an ever greater disadvantage.

Such a situation is not unique in history. We find similar conditions pertaining in many societies. Even our own society was once acquainted with such a situation (long ago and in a completely different form). As I have already suggested, the way of thinking introduced into sociology by Bourdieu will be of great assistance in illuminating the functional difficulties of such an economy. And merely to ask why is to identify at a stroke the main problem that stands before us at the turn of the post-totalitarian period.

Bourdieu came from the tradition of cultural anthropology. His theoretical constructions are based on observations of primitive societies, where money plays a minor role, the state is weak, the law only applies to certain members, and all commercial and indeed social transactions are carried out on the basis of a member's "word of honour", without being enshrined in a written contract. The parties to such a transaction must remember its contents. Quite whose memory of the agreement applies in the event of a dispute is decided by the social status of the participants to the transaction: there is no written law nor independent court of appeal. Social status is not based on competence, as a meritocratic explanation of modern societies would have us believe, nor is it based on assets, as understood by modern economic theory, but on the extent of its clientship and their ritualised prestige, i.e. on their social and symbolic capital.

It is no easy task to identify such a society at the close of the 20th century. Bourdieu laid the groundwork for his career as a cultural anthropologist by living among the Kabyle, a primitive tribe in the remote, semi-desert conditions of southern Algiers. On the basis of observations of their society, he created a remarkable sociological theory that has had a huge influence on the interpretation of modern societies by contemporary sociologists.

And now, perhaps, the ordinary Czech reader is beginning to understand why the Kabyle might be of interest to us.

There are of course many fundamental differences. However, I believe the model proposed by Bourdieu is deserving of our attention. So let us first look at how Kabyle society operates.

The basic economic transaction among the Kabyle is not a sale, but a gift. This is due both to the unreliability of the currency, and to the special relationship the tribe has with profit, a point that will be discussed later. The gift, however, is only an external, socially presented form of that which is in reality an exchange. The receiver has an obligation to the giver, and, in due course, will repay the gift with a counter-gift, while carefully concealing the fact that this is also an exchange. The receiver, too, presents what they are offering as a true gift, i.e. as a selfless expression of affection and generosity. Not only must they not make any mention of the prior obligation, but in the interests of concealing the true nature of the transaction they must offer a gift, the value of which corresponds to the outstanding receivable, without being *exactly the same* as that of which it represents repayment. Were this rule not to be observed, it would be insulting, since it would imply that the recipient expects a corresponding compensation. However, over the long term, the sum of all exchanges must balance out. But because they keep no written records (if only because the Kabyle are for the most part illiterate), this places great demands on the memory and commitment of the parties to the transaction.

"The theoretical construction which retrospectively projects the counter-gift into the project of the gift does not only have the effect of producing mechanical sequences of obligatory acts from the risky but necessary improvisation of everyday strategies – strategies which owe their infinite complexity to the fact that the giver's undeclared calculation has to reckon with the receiver's undeclared calculation, and hence satisfy his expectations without appearing to know what they are." Bourdieu (1977: 171).

Complicated, certainly. But all of us, even in modern societies, negotiate such matters. We need not return to the Kabyle for an example. Bourdieu shows how in France, a doctor who is examined by a specialist in another field will not pay for his treatment: it would be deemed a faux pas worthy of pistols at dawn to accept a fee for a collegial favour. However, a small gift is deemed appropriate. It need not have the exact price normally charged for such an examination, but it must not differ conspicuously from said price. Meanwhile, the outward facade that I will not profit from a colleague's illness has been preserved.

The ritual slaughtering of a pig, as practiced in Czech villages since time immemorial, is another example of such a *gift economy*. A substantial portion of every pig slaughtered is distributed to various neighbours. However, these neighbours also slaughter pigs, but at different times, and also distribute a substantial amount to their neighbours, with the result that the entire village has fresh sausages all winter, no one loses out, and everyone feels (and is) generous. It's better than a refrigerator. No money circulates between them, no accounts are held (only in the memory, unreported), and yet the entire system works, balancing economic surpluses and deficits.

The *archaic economy*, as Polanyi (1944) called this system, is not, however, limited to the market for goods. It also applies to the labour market. Just as the market for goods is realised as the (non-)exchange of gifts, so the labour market is realised as the (non-)exchange of favours and acts of kindness. Let us leave the Kabyle for now and relocate to a Czech village. My neighbour is putting a new roof on his house, and so I help throw up the tiles. Any thought of payment is out of the question. Likewise, he repairs my water pressure tank as a favour, because he is a good neighbour and, in addition, an electrician. Even moving up a level on the labour market, it is still the case that I take no money for offering my neighbour's daughter a job in my company, and I am prepared to wait years until he is able to help my son get into a particular school. These are all favours and acts of kindness. However, the sum total of all of these transactions must be balanced and the calculations must not be ostentatious (which does not mean that they are not to be seen). It is the performative selflessness of one's own actions that makes it possible to pretend to accept the actions of others as selfless. This creates a climate on the market that has led to the archaic economy also being called the *goodwill economy*, though perhaps more accurately it should be called the economy of *declared* goodwill.

In the case of the Kabyle, strict adherence to the principle of selflessness changes both their approach to work and the very nature of that work. Bourdieu observed of the Kabyle, that

"[A]ctivity is as much a duty of communal life as an economic necessity. What is valued is activity for its own sake, regardless of its strictly economic function, inasmuch as it is regarded as appropriate to the function of the person doing it. Only the application of categories alien to peasant experience (those imposed by economic domination and the generalisation of monetary exchanges) brings up the distinction between the technical aspect and the ritual or symbolic aspect of agricultural activity. The distinction between productive and unproductive work or between profitable and unprofitable work is unknown: the ancient economy knows only the opposition between the idler who fails in his social duty and the worker who performs his socially defined proper function, whatever the product of his effort." (Bourdieu 1977: 175)

This ethnographic description of a Kabyle village inevitably brings to mind the socialist work brigades of the communist era.

As I have already said, the second characteristic of the social world of a Kabyle village, with its archaic goodwill economy, is the fact that *profit has a bad name*. The openly declared guiding principle is selflessness. Under the harsh conditions endured by a tribe living on the edge of a desert (or the wretchedness of society following the civil war in Russia), this is understandable. Resources are limited and such a society comes up against these limits on a daily basis. However, within these limits the profit of one is the loss of another, necessarily and manifestly. A high degree of solidarity and altruism thus arises naturally, in the form of an all-binding ideal.

However, selflessness as the basic principle of societal organisation simply does not work in a more complex society.[30] All the larger societies that we know of are based on the unequal distribution of power (wealth, influence, knowledge, etc.). Those who have less wealth do everything in their power to ensure that things do not remain this way, especially in a situation in which resources are so

---

30 Selflessness as the guiding organisational principle is only successful at the lowest developmental stage, in small groups lost in a wilderness, of whom Polanyi uses the term "primitive economy".

limited that to be at the bottom of the pile means not surviving. Those who, on the other hand, have more, do everything to ensure that things remain this way, and opt for an active defence strategy. Thus everyone *seeks profit*, whatever the ruling ideology might claim to the contrary. Archaic economies soon end up with pharaohs owning vast wealth and the lowly comrade scraping a living. The dominant discourse of selflessness only serves to cover up the existing reality.

It would appear that the limited power of money and an ideology of selflessness and solidarity must be an insurmountable obstacle to the creation of great wealth and power. They are indeed an obstacle, and the way that archaic economies managed to overcome this barrier is one of the most admirable feats of the human spirit prior to the invention of money.

What fascinated Bourdieu most about the Kabyle was the ritualisation of their daily lives. Behaviour governed by ritual gives precedence to the criterion of "correctness" over the criterion of best outcome, or, as we might say, the criterion of the rational. In the realm of the material reproduction of society, ritualised behaviour follows patterns of "correctness" even when they result in a worse outcome, e.g. when they lead to lower productivity, or when they result in loss rather than profit. In societies with an archaic economy, this does not have to be deemed a fundamental flaw, because profit as such is socially taboo. However, the real profit that flows to all involved in such behaviour (since otherwise there would be no reason for them to participate) is of an intangible kind. It is *symbolic*. It resides in the fact that such behaviour confirms on a daily basis the mutual social status of those involved, and reproduces the governing relationships of domination and exploitation in a moneyless economy. Those who acquire such profit conceal it carefully.

This does not involve only, or even mainly, the ritualisation of critical moments, of ceremonial or special occasions, notwithstanding the fact that there are more of these in an archaic society than in modern societies and they are more ostentatious and energy intensive. When 19th-century travellers pushing their way into the interior of Africa described the festivals and gatherings they saw, the ostentatious destruction of precious objects by powerful chiefs in front of invited guests, the feasts that exhausted all supplies and were followed by hunger, i.e. all these exotic and plainly "irrational" customs, they had no explanation for them other than the childish nature of the natives.

However, ritualisation has its own deep rationality. Bourdieu reads its presence in the daily habitus of the life of a Kabyle village, and points to its social function. Its aim is to reproduce established social relations. It overcomes the fundamental obstacle to the establishment and maintenance of great power and wealth in society, where in many ordinary situations money has a dubious value, profit is illegitimate, and where power, given the weakness of the state and to all intents and purposes the non-existence of a police force, is based mainly on an ability to mobilise sufficient support during times of crisis. Power is defined by the size of the mobilised clientele or personal support network, and not by a fat bank account or the legitimacy of social status guaranteed by the state, a legitimacy the rights to which can be enforced by judicial and police powers.

Institutionalised ritualisation creates *symbolic capital.* To the outside observer, symbolic capital appears as a measure of prestige, and in a gift economy it presents itself as distinctly *non*-economic capital: hence the exalted concept of honour. However, in addition to a social function, prestige clearly possesses an economic function. Given the weakness of the coercive institutions of the state and law, and the verbal, tacit form of all agreements, it is the prestige of the parties involved that guarantees all economic transactions. This is extremely important, since, in the competition for limited resources, the basis of the reproduction of established social relations in societies with an archaic economy (in contrast to societies with a primitive economy) is clearly wealth and an advantageous position within a system characterised by the unequal redistribution of resources; this is merely carefully concealed. The institution of the gift in such an economy is not a dysfunctional anomaly of the social order in question, but, on the contrary, a fundamental mechanism for overcoming the contradiction between the illegitimacy of profit and a social structure based on great inequality: it conceals the true state of affairs in order to make said state of affairs possible. And it does so whatever the cost.

Bourdieu writes that behind the theoretical construction of the gift is concealed

"the institutionally organized and guaranteed misrecognition which is the basis of gift exchange and, perhaps, of all the symbolic labour intended to transmute, by the sincere fiction of a disinterested exchange, the inevitable, and inevitably interested relations imposed by kinship, neighbourhood, or work, into elective relations of reciprocity, through the sincere fiction of a disinterested exchange, and, more profoundly, at transforming arbitrary relations of exploitation (of woman by man, younger brother by elder brother, the young by the elders) into durable relations, grounded in nature. In the work of reproducing established relations – feasts, ceremonies, exchange of gifts, visits or courtesies and, above all, marriages – which is no less vital to the existence of the group than the reproduction of the economic bases of its existence, the labour required to conceal the function of the exchanges is as important as the labour needed to perform this function." (1977: 171)

Such an economy is as non-transparent (intentionally) as it is unnecessarily costly (of necessity). The simple reproduction of established relationships requires those who have the greatest interest in them to invest a disproportionate amount. Their main losses are incurred from the need to disguise what it is they are actually doing.

But even those at the bottom of the heap, who genuinely have no interest in reproducing these relationships, must pay. Whether they want to be or not, they find themselves being recruited as actors in rituals. It is of little consolation to them to know that there are few people whose position in the pecking order is so low that there is no one beneath them, and that they themselves will sometimes act as the organiser of rituals. However, even as a simple actor, the ordinary Kabyle, led by the rule that if you have to do it, at least pretend you're enjoying it, occasionally derives something positive from their participation in rituals: at least they get to eat for free.

And here the two reasons come together that finally led those who did not belong to the socialist establishment, but lived with it in an uneasy truce for many years, during which time many families actually settled in quite comfortably, to make their way to the public squares.

As we have already seen, the first reason was purely material. The value of money plummeted and the system of shopping around by deploying social capital made increasing demands on time, resources and energy. The second reason was of an intangible, symbolic character. The population was simply fed up with the pointless ritualisation of everyday life, not to mention the obligatorily enthusiastic celebrations of state holidays. There were fewer and fewer opportunities to eat for free, and the ruling class, given the illegitimacy of profit and the impossibility of relying on economic capital guaranteed by the state and the law, became more and more neurotic regarding its symbolic capital and stubbornly insistent on rituals. It could not be otherwise, since it, too, was held captive by the system.

The young generation especially found the reverence paid the Communist Party difficult to come to terms with. They were not in a position to know that, in an archaic economy, where power is based on symbolic capital, it was simply not the done thing to ridicule the establishment. And that such economies must necessarily have a law making it a crime to satirise the president and must be able to send someone to prison for a political anecdote and lock up a playwright for harming the interests of the state abroad by sending out essays and plays that could not be published in his own country. And that such economies must be able to persecute long-haired singers who make fun of big issues in small halls in the company of their peers. For all of these activities undermine the honour of the ruling class. And this honour must be defended carefully, because it is symbolic capital, the basis of legitimacy and power.

The truth is the vast majority of the population did not give a fig about long-haired singers. But they were plagued by the relentless ritualisation of everyday life, the mind-numbingly meaningless propaganda slogans hanging in shop windows, public buildings described in terms of their noble mission, the endlessly finessed plans for political re-education, the humiliating ritual visits to the VUML or the IPV, PŠM or the MLP,[31] and children at kindergarten being befuddled by Lenin...

At work, too, ritualisation reached an intolerable degree. The academic community still engaged in the carousel of rituals involved in defending state, departmental and faculty dissertations, interim and preliminary reports, and introductory research reports, while a courteous expert would hold their nose and engage in ritual candidatures for research posts, the main part of which involved opulent banquets for the holders of symbolic titles he generally held in boundless contempt. In the end, everyone got drunk, but not enough to loosen their tongues. Not only the domain of research, but all other crafts underwent the rituals of production meetings, work meetings, the compilation of plans, implementation of plans, modification of plans, the monitoring of key performance indicators,

---

31 It will not be long before we have forgotten what these initials used to refer to. So for the sake of posterity: VUML – the Evening University of Marxism-Leninism; IPV – Ideological and Political Education; PŠM – Political Team Training; MLP – Marxist-Leninist Preparation.

the introduction of innovation... everything was empty, stupid and mortifying.

Even the party cadre blanched when they realised that for the rest of their lives there was no escape from the endless merry-go-round of monthly meetings, annual meetings, committee meetings, commission assemblies, approval of minutes, scrutiny of resolutions, approval of resolutions... It sounds like black comedy when the modern version of the Communist Party claims that seventy-five percent of its members were active in the Velvet Revolution because it represented their interests. But in essence the claim is true. (But then gallows humour tends to hit the mark: this is its dark side).

The archaic means of reproducing power by means of the ritualised, everyday self-abasement of its subjects, who thus demonstrated their mobilisability while established social relations were symbolically confirmed, dissolved. By the end of the 1980s, even the most affluent greengrocer, while dutifully placing the slogan "Workers of the world unite!" in his shop window, would rather the same workers simply tax him. He would happily have surrendered part of his profit to a union if it meant cutting the crap.[32]

---

32 Sometime back in the 1970s, I once had an entire evening spoiled by the host, who spent the whole time moaning about his fate and cursing the regime. He was a millionaire from south Moravia who had rented Mikulov castle for his son's wedding and had a white dinner suit specially tailored for him. He had three cars parked in the garage of his new villa, where there was a television in the bathroom. When I tried to point out to Mr Moneybags (employed as procurement officer at the STS [the Machine Tractor Station, a state enterprise for the ownership and maintenance of agricultural machinery used on collective farms: t/n] that under no other circumstances would he have made as much money, with a monopoly on prices and no taxes, and asked him what he lacked, he dismayed me by answering – *freedom*. At the time I didn't understand, though I now know he was referring to the legitimacy of his status. He had had enough of his ambivalent station in life: on the one hand, he was a winemaker blessed with god-given talent, a highly respected rich country man with a flourishing business; on the other, he had to cower, avert his gaze and bribe everyone around, from his less successful neighbours and local PS VB [*Pomocná stráž Veřejné bezpečnosti* or Auxiliary Security Guard, an organisation set up to maintain public order: t/n], to suspicious characters from the surrounding district and region. From time to time a T 613 [a luxury rear-wheel drive car manufactured by the Czechoslovak company Tatra mostly used by government officials: t/n] with a Prague registration plate would draw up in front of his wine cellar and he would be informed that his wine was even drunk at Prague Castle.

2.

I hope I have managed to sketch out the causes that led the ordinary person to reject vigorously a system in which, at the end of the day, he wasn't *so* badly off. At present, many people regret the demise of the old practices and make pathetic attempts to hold on to a socialist way of life after the collapse of the old regime, even though they do not belong among those who deemed it their own.

The more difficult task will be to justify my opinion that the collapse was so smooth because ultimately not only those at the bottom had an interest in changing the system, but those at the top too, the key stakeholders – indeed, this latter group especially. But what the heck, let's give it a go.

To begin with, let us observe that the key stakeholders, i.e. those at the top of the pile, the families of the powerful, were basically those who were able to exercise a right of disposition (to reach binding decisions) on the level of the economy that is now to become subject to "mass privatisation"[33]. They were the communist "large owners". As is common in all economies on this level, their ownership was often of a very abstract character. In general, they shared their assets, creating complex and hierarchised networks of co-participation and mutually connected and controlled competencies. However, the basic features of the ownership relations were as follows: they had exclusive, albeit collective rights of disposition over large state assets, and were able to invoke coercive force if anyone called into question the legitimacy of that right. When, on the other hand, I speak of small and ordinary families, I am referring to families that lived and

He could be toppled at any moment. His power lacked any institutional support whatsoever, his only genuinely liquid capital was symbolic. Notwithstanding their outwardly congenial character, most of the gatherings held in his wine cellar were ritualistic. A sudden fall from grace was by no means unimaginable. Things happened. These days, when I hear the word freedom, I sometimes think back to this man.

[33] The aim of which was to privatise medium and large enterprises in the industrial sector as part of the transformation of the Czechoslovak economy: t/n.

did business in a sphere that is now to be the subject of small-scale privatisation[34] and used their economic power in the manner described above. This division is somewhat crude and simplistic,[35] and I can well imagine the reaction of some of my colleagues. Nevertheless, it has a tradition in sociological theories of class dichotomy and more modern theories of dominion and the new class.

Empirically, such dichotomisation is firmly based on a uniquely reliable indicator: the records in the nomenklatura. No one denies that the principal difference was between those who were part of the nomenklatura and those who were not. (In this respect the loss of the nomenklatura files has had a similar impact on sociology in this country as the fire at the Library of Alexandria had on classical education.)

Digging the grave of the *ancien régime* during the French Revolution was not begun by the people. Historians agree that the demand for change was first made by the nobility, who were extremely unhappy with the situation as it pertained: things simply got a little out of hand. But could history really repeat itself in this way?

A reader who has not accepted the indirect parallel I have offered between the organisation of the old order in Czechoslovakia and that of Kabyle society must be convinced that, at the very least, I am guilty of the most egregious exaggeration. Even at the close of the

---

34 One of the first stages by which the entire process of privatisation was initiated in Czechoslovakia after 1989, the aim of which, inter alia, was to re-establish small enterprises, of which there were practically none, and to transfer ownership of retail outlets and service providers from the state to private parties: t/n.

35 However, the working-class clans do not fall within this category, even though it might at first sight seem as though they would. They were embedded in the "sphere of small-scale privatisation", either through casual work on the informal economy performed by the breadwinner, or through the employment of women in the sphere of goods and services. If not, they were genuinely socially marginalised. Furthermore, we must not forget that more than half of our workers were villagers, who, by means of the natural small-holding economy and within a network of small rural craftsmen, created a by no means negligible part of the production of our second economy. "Everybody has work on the side, Professor," a neighbour told me when I moved into my new weekend cottage in Kulířov.

post-totalitarian era, they will proclaim loudly, our police state was anything but a weak state, and, whatever else our society lacked, it was not coercive power.

Oh yes it was. However, its weakness did not reside in the fact that it received insufficient funding. The problem was that its system was hopelessly obsolete, and productivity so desperately low, that in the end there was simply not enough to go around. As the dissatisfaction of small families grew and the discomfiture of the large ones intensified, demands on power intensified and its limits began to appear critical.

The incursion of Soviet power into Central Europe at the end of the World War II resulted in the creation of very specific circumstances. Stalin and his successors built an empire through a series of aggressive acts centrally controlled from Moscow. In some parts of an empire that was to stretch from Ulaanbaatar to Prague and from Tallinn to Tbilisi, given the survival of the institutions of a traditional society with limited literacy and a primitive market, the introduction of a command economy and centralised political system represented a modernising act. However, in the newly seized territories in the west [i.e. in central Europe: t/n], the implementation of such measures was clearly regressive and led to a drop in economic productivity and social decline.

However, the rationality of subjugation took precedence over the rationality of production. Achieving systemic homogeneity became the absolute imperative. This mattered more in some places, less in others. In Central Asia, the introduction of real socialism entered a socially unoccupied space. The construction of centralised hyperstructures took place over the structures of traditional local societies, which ended up in a sense forming the natural and hierarchically rational base of the new system and perhaps even had some chance in the next phase to flow into it and be transformed into a new quality. The new system arose in direct interaction with these traditional structures and shared a common logic with them.[36]

The situation was different in Central Europe. The implementation of the same system within the systems of modern states and advanced economies already constituted on this level required the destruction of these hyperstructures and their institutions. After a huge and sometimes bloody effort, this was more or less achieved. It brought with it an unintended and paradoxical consequence: the reconstitution, or perhaps the resuscitation, of well-nigh defunct traditional and local elementary systems, organised above all on the principle of mutual support networks that took the form of clans, often family based. However, these systems were not (as they had originally been) the outcome of a thousand years of natural development, but arose as a consequence of the invasion of a foreign culture, unintentionally and on a top-down basis. They could not develop the whole of their traditional institutional network (e.g. a morality based on shared religious beliefs, a patriarchy based on the traditional household, social control based on immobility, etc.). And last but not least, they were reconstituted within the context of modern production, communication and education, which even the new system had a vital interest in maintaining (weapons for further aggression could not be produced traditionally). For all of these reasons, a strange blend of traditionalism and modernity of unique scope and quality emerged in Central Europe.

Initially, the implementation of some of the principles underpinning archaic economies did not meet with strong resistance even in Central Europe. Not even here had the somewhat naive albeit deeply ingrained desire for traditional society been consigned to the dustbin of history, but was generally manifest in an unacknowledged

36 However, pressure on the collapse of the Soviet empire from the Asian republics too shows that not even this opportunity appears to have been taken. On the other hand, it is significant that the strongest support on the part of local elites for conservative Soviet centralism comes from certain Central Asian republics.

nostalgia. The pursuit of constant material self-enrichment as an incentive to participate in economic enterprise *institutionally imposed* by capitalism undoubtedly eroded the social and communal life of human communities, which lost much of their intimacy and warmth in comparison with traditional society. And so there was a great temptation, especially for humanist intellectuals, to attempt to restore the benefits of classical *Gemeinschaft* and revive these elements in a society organised around the state rather than the contract, or at least to try to conceive of a kind of amalgam of traditionalism and modernity that *would possess the benefits of both.* (The passion for folk song, folkloric ornament and ethnographic clubs in the 1950s was no coincidence.)

Sociology has created theories of modernisation, but lacks a theory of de-modernisation. However, without such a theory it will not be possible to create a theory of re-modernisation, and that which is taking place before our eyes will remain unexplained.[37]

These days it may be clear to us that the basic problem regarding this strange combination of the archaic and modern economy was that it implanted in a modern means of production a blurred category of ownership from the archaic economy, took from it the social taboo of profit, and thus obscured the relations of dominance, exploitation and social inequality, which was the main outcome and

---

37 Since its beginnings at the start of the 19th century in France, the whole of sociology has been conceived of as a theory of modernisation. Special theories of modernisation then experienced a second youth quite recently in the optimistic 1950s and 1960s. It is true that things became more complicated in Europe. However, modernisation theory was fascinated by progress and its problems in the Third World. It seemed to occur to no one at the time that the opposite process, i.e. the regression of modern social structures to traditional structures, could be socially significant, even though this was taking place right in the middle of Europe on a huge scale and in front of everyone's eyes. It was only certain of the shocks of the 1970s and 1980s (e.g. the victory of fundamentalism in Iran) that drew attention to the fact that development is not a one-way street and dampened the optimism of modernists. However, the theory of de-modernisation is still threadbare and has difficulty explaining the mode of development *Shag vpered, dva shaga nazad* [1904; Lenin. One Step forward, Two Steps Back: t/n].

unacknowledged goal of those who took upon themselves the practical realisation of the entire operation.

The inevitable outcome was to shift the focus of social life from the market of economic capital to the recreated, or, better still, many times expanded market of social and symbolic capital, with all the consequences ensuing from this archaic organisation of the logic and economy of social life. One of the most important of these consequences was the mutual permeation and, ultimately, transformation in modern states of already emancipated spheres of the economy, governance, politics and ideology into a single whole.

The achievement of the goal of permanently obscuring the relations of dominance and exploitation using archaic practices within the context of modern production was, however, a social utopia that had no hope of being realised, even if displayed initial signs of success. We have already described how small families gradually saw through the true character of ownership and intuitively understood the convertibility of the capital of power, economic ownership and symbolic domination achieved by means of the complete expropriation of the public semantic space and the extensive ritualisation of public life. We have described how they participated in creeping reprivatisation by means of their "small-scale gradual reprivatisation" of the networks of commerce and services, how they were aware of the limits of this re-expropriation, and how keenly they perceived the existence of the antagonism of group interests between themselves and large establishment owners.

A basic element that large owners had to take into account when formulating strategy was nationalisation of the economy. Fragmented and competing enterprises were stripped of their owners and subjected to central control, and the entire economic sphere lost the autochthonous dynamic that had been so difficult to calculate. The state held the economy firmly in its hands. Everyone was technically speaking a state employee, and anyone who had any decision-making power had been placed in their position by bureaucratic appointment.

At first glance, this boosted the power of the state considerably. However, was it genuinely the people working in the state administration who oversaw the national economy? Or, more precisely, was the state genuinely the institution in which ownership rights to national assets were realised? For the Czech reader it is virtually unnecessary to recapitulate the facts that demonstrated the exact opposite. So let us be as brief as possible.

It was the Communist Party that determined the foundations of the long-term and most momentous economic strategies. It made no secret of the fact. It reached such decisions as an organisation of imperial power, formulated them as motions passed at its congresses, and supervised their implementation through the whole of its apparat. The only conceivable government programme was as follows:

WE SHALL IMPLEMENT THE CONCLUSIONS OF THE UMPTEENTH CONGRESS OF THE CZECHOSLOVAK COMMUNIST PARTY!

However, tactical decision-making and, of course, many specialised day-to-day decisions, remained in the hands of the administrative apparat of state power. Individual officials, beginning with the prime minister and ending with the lowliest regional secretary, were completely in the hands of the Party, which appointed them and could recall them at any time. The prime minister was selected by the executive committee and the deciding influence on the choice of a particular person depended on the balance of power between individual cliques and lobbyists in the apparat of the Central Committee. Every prime minister was a member of the Central Committee, drew up regular reports for it and fell in line with its decisions. His ministers, too, were in a similar situation in respect of the relevant departments of the state apparat. Lower down the ladder came their deputies and union leaders, in the economic sphere the general directors of individual sectors and the managers who answered to them, in the regional authorities the secretaries and senior civil servants of the regional, district and local national committees, and in the non-production sphere all management personnel, including university rectors and deans; even a bishop's consecration was subject to veto by the Party when it no longer had at its disposal the appropriate rituals to ordain him itself.

Everyone was appointed and recalled by the Party: not by their superiors or even by means of a vote among their subordinates. Any more significant exercise of state rights of ownership was controlled by the secretariats, the departments for industry, trade, state bodies, education… All genuinely important managerial decisions were reached by the secretariat: some at meetings of the relevant departments, but many during whispered conversations in the corridors of power. A director who had decided to replace his deputy had to submit a proposal and obtain approval "in the apparat". However, before asking for such approval, the unwritten rule was that he must hold "consultations" as to whether this was the appropriate step. This procedure became institutionalised, even though, it goes without saying, its rules were never recorded in writing. The degree to which it had become formalised and routine was such that, prior to the "proper" consultations being held, the procedure was first subject to informal, personal consultations as to whether formal, impersonal consultations should take place.

The state bureaucracy appeared to be all-powerful. From outside and from afar, that is. But this was an optical illusion caused by its pervasiveness. In fact, it played a purely instrumental role. It "refined" decisions and implemented the resolutions reached elsewhere. Everyone knew that nothing whatsoever could take place without the approval of the Party. The fundamental source of frustration for authentic bureaucrats was the violation of at least two pillars of their power. Firstly, the basic principle of the functioning of bureaucratic systems, namely, that a regular civil servant does not take instructions from anyone other than their direct superior, and when making decisions at their level follows universal rather than partisan considerations, and does not offer information regarding their actions to anyone other than their superior (and above all to no one outside their organisation) – this principle was completely torn apart. The Party intervened directly on all levels in decision-making with no consideration for the hierarchical structure of a department: this applied to both the civil service and the management of nationalised industries. This intervention was oriented mainly toward partisan and not universal considerations, and the acquisition of insight into all mechanisms of the state administration and details of economic life was one of the privileges taken for granted by Party apparatchiks.

Secondly, in modern societies, the state has an absolute monopoly on physical force in the public square. Coercive institutions, namely the army, criminal law and the police, are constituted as components of the state apparatus. The government wields socially legitimate executive power and governs these institutions as instruments of that power. The second fundamental breach of the proper functioning of the administrative apparatus of the modern state resided in the fact that coercive institutions were in fact exempt from its authority. The army and the police force were not run by the government, but by the Party. Both the army and police force were permeated by a system of Party organisations and their instructors, to whom the formal chain of command was answerable for each of their decisions.

All of this (along with several other features of the system that need not occupy our attention here) meant that the state *de facto* lost almost all of the independent power that states have in modern societies, and became merely the facade or tool of the real power, which resided elsewhere. Powerful as it appeared, it was in fact a woefully weak state.

In reality, however, everything was both far more complicated and much simpler. The real helplessness of the police and their instrumental status in relation to the Party apparat was not so clear cut, or at least not as far as the political police were concerned (the Party had the criminal investigation and transport police departments as much on a string as the courts and other state bodies). Here was the source of a real threat to power. However, it was and is difficult to decide whether the Party ruled the interior ministry or the interior ministry the Party, since in reality they overlapped to such an extent that they were mutually indistinguishable. And this applied to the rest of the state administration and nationalised economy. The board of every district committee was the venue for meetings of the following: the director of the most important local factory, the secretary of the district national committee, a colonel or major from the interior ministry or the army, several party secretaries, the chairman of the unions, the district prosecutor... Those a rung down met at the plenary of the district committee, at the instructor corps, the teaching group... various heads were present and the Party operated for them as a club for bosses. It was impossible to hold any kind of managerial position and not be a member of this club. *All* of the power components of social life were inseparably connected by personnel unions: the Party and state apparats, economic management and coercive units.

However, this did not involve only personal unions and mutually interconnected clans. Socially more significant was the fact that all the elements of social life were functionally unified: the coercive system occasionally assisted in meeting the economic plan, which in turn operated as an extension of the coercive system; the education system also oversaw the potato harvest and held children hostage in order to blackmail parents; and the state administration merged with the party apparat to such an extent that it was ultimately unclear as to whether the president was the head of state or chairman of the Party...

The existence of relatively autonomous spheres with their own, at least functionally intersecting, external mechanisms – one of the key differences between a modern and archaic society – was of course absent from this system, or at the very least the existence of the "leading role" principle was critically weakened.

This was how the first generation involved in the building of socialism conceived of the state and society. Considering that this was a system that, wherever established, operated in a hostile social space and in general under conditions in which acute tension reduced the demands on the economy and civil administration to a minimum, it does not appear as absurd to us as it might look in retrospect. However, it suited every subsequent generation of the establishment less and less, and its weaknesses became more and more pronounced as the level of emergency and internal threat declined, the life of economic and social institutions became more sophisticated, and the demands made upon them were greater and more differentiated.[38]

38 Even a failed attempt at reform from 1968 can now be viewed with hindsight as an attempt to emancipate individual spheres of society, especially the state and the economy, from the archaic omniscience and indiscriminate homogeneity of the political system of a socialist society. It is no coincidence that the initiators of the 1968 uprising were established communists, themselves representatives of the system. At the beginning, everyone who aspired to participate in the building of a new society (i.e. participate in power) entered the Party and attempted to become involved in its assets and especially in its apparat. However, gradually the more intelligent, repelled by the alienation, emptiness and brutality of power, which had become an end in itself, seized every opportunity and moved from there to managerial positions in economic functions or to the state apparat. They got to carry out more meaningful work, and though this meant relinquishing a degree of power, the nature of the power they now wielded was more real. In terms of the ruling form of capital, the transition from symbolic to economic power meant their voluntary marginalisation, though in reality their modernisation. But as regards the problems of modern production and the state on the Procrustean bed of archaic regime, problems that someone in a managerial position of the economic or state apparat had to resolve on a daily basis, they felt increasingly uncomfortable that their stupider comrades, whom they had left behind in the political apparat of the Party, were speaking over them. And they always had the last word, for heaven's sake! They relied on disgruntled intellectuals, disappointed that the coveted humanising effect of socialism had not appeared, and rebelled. Hence the call for economic reform. This was not about worker participation in management, as Šik put it, but about paralysing the participation of apparatchiks in economic power. And the Party apparat was not so stupid that they didn't recognise it. This was what they lived for. With an archaic (Soviet-Russian) empire breathing down your neck, you did not have to wait long for the outcome. The increasing opposition to the modernisers of '68, who were reproached for having wanted nothing less than socialism once again, but this time around

But before looking in more detail at the weaknesses of this system, as experienced by the establishment in recent years, here is a lengthier quote from Bourdieu, again on the topic of the Kabyles:

"In societies which have no 'self-regulating market' (in Karl Polanyi's sense), no educational system, no juridical apparatus, and no State, relations of domination can be set up and maintained only at the cost of strategies which must be endlessly renewed, because the conditions required for a *mediated, lasting appropriation* of other agents' labour, services, or homage have not been brought together. By contrast, domination no longer needs to be exerted in a direct, personal way when it is entailed in possession of the means (economic or cultural capital) of appropriating the mechanisms of the field of production and the field of cultural production, which tend to assure their own reproduction by their very functioning, independently of any deliberate intervention by the agents. So it is in the degree of objectification of the accumulated social capital that one finds the basis of all the pertinent differences between the modes of domination: that is, very schematically, between, on the one hand, social universes in which relations of domination are made, unmade, and remade in and by the interactions between persons, and on the other hand, social formations in which, mediated by objective, institutionalised mechanisms, such as those producing and guaranteeing the distribution of 'titles' (titles of nobility, deeds of possession, academic degrees, etc.), relations of domination have the opacity and permanence of things and escape the grasp of individual consciousness and power. Objectification guarantees the permanence and cumulativity of material and symbolic acquisitions which can then subsist without the agents having to recreate them continuously and in their entirety by deliberate action; but, because the profits of these institutions are the object of differential appropriation, objectification also and inseparably ensures the reproduction

reformed, drew on period rhetoric and concealed the essence of the problem, or did not understand it. "Socialism" was simply a slogan on a facade. In reality, this was an attempt to modernise the archaic social system imposed upon us from outside by means of the emancipation of the spheres of social life.

of the structure of the distribution of the capital which, in its various forms, is the precondition for such appropriation, and in so doing, reproduces the structure of the relations of domination and dependence.

Paradoxically, it is precisely because there exist relatively autonomous fields, functioning in accordance with rigorous mechanisms capable of imposing their necessity on the agents, that those who are in a position to command these mechanisms and to appropriate the material and/or symbolic profits accruing from their functioning are able to *dispense with* strategies aimed *expressly* (which does not mean manifestly) and directly (i.e. without being mediated by the mechanisms) at the domination of individuals, a domination which in this case is the condition of the appropriation of the material and symbolic profits of their labour. The saving is a real one, because strategies designed to establish or maintain lasting relations of dependence are generally very expensive in terms of material goods (as in the potlatch or in charitable acts), services, or simply *time*; which is why, by a paradox constitutive of this mode of domination, the means eat up the end, and the actions necessary to ensure the continuation of power themselves help to weaken it." (Bourdieu 1977: 184)[39]

Of course, the situation in Central Europe was fundamentally different from the one Bourdieu studied in the Kabyle villages, and it would be dangerous and misleading to draw too close a parallel. The education system, for example, was the outcome of many years' development in our countries, and there was a high level of scholarship. Illiteracy, one of the structural features of Kabyle society, was virtually unknown here. The police service in Central Europe, too, was the outcome of a tradition stretching back several centuries; the municipalities and the state had long ago taken it upon themselves to guarantee the safety of their citizens rather than rely on the dagger at the waist and membership of a dreaded clan. And other

---

39 Quoted from Pierre Bourdieu: *Outline of a Theory of Practice*, transl. Richard Nice, Cambridge: Cambridge University Press, 1977, 184: transl.

institutions enjoyed an incomparably higher degree of social maturity too. Nevertheless, it became increasingly apparent that in the amalgam of archaic and modern government, "the means eat up the end, and the actions necessary to ensure the continuation of power themselves help to weaken it". (Bourdieu 1990b, 131)

Some of the differences, striking at first glance, were in reality not so pronounced. And these tended to be the differences that mattered the most. I have already indicated how, under the conditions pertaining even in Czechoslovakia, the real power of state institutions was paradoxically drained, and its social weight critically reduced. As for the legal system, we might similarly infer, by merely recalling the well known facts of the matter, that, though externally it resembled similar legal systems of modern societies, in its practical functioning and especially through the social weight of law, all that remained was a husk, and even this lost its socially constitutive power. The exercise of the law in this country resembled European law only inasmuch as the cat in the canary's cage resembles the canary that it devours.

The exercise of coercive power as an instrument of the state also encountered surprising problems. It was often forced to resort to highly archaic, officialising strategies. In a modern society, when someone breaks the law through a political act, they are fined or imprisoned. Full stop. Our powers-that-be, when they wanted to exert coercive force against their political opponents (or among themselves), had to invest huge amounts of capital in order to create a scandal around their opponent, by means of which they symbolically acquired official interest. As in the case of the Kabyles, locking up a signatory of Charta 77 (or their own Secretary General) did not suffice: it was still necessary to make of them an *amahbul*.[40]

---

40 Bourdieu described the situation amongst the Kabyles thus: "Strategies aimed at producing 'regular' practices are one category, among others, of officializing strategies, the object of which is to transmute 'egoistic', private, particular interests… into disinterested, collective, publicly avowable, legitimate interests. In the absence of political institutions endowed with an effective

It was in the economic sphere that the situation pertaining in Czechoslovakia most resembled Kabyle society. The institution of profit was taboo in both societies. As amongst the Kabyles, economic subjects pretended that the endeavour to enrich themselves was alien to them. I am not an economist and will therefore refrain from going into details. However, the deep decline in the level of contractual guarantees of these transactions, coupled with a drop in the weight of the institution of law and state, a change in the proportion of economic and non-economic coercion linked to the relativisation of the power of money, a sovereignty stripped of the institution of individual, transparent, legally guaranteed (private) ownership, which had lost the support of the state... historians of political economy still have a lot of work to do if they are to explain how it all worked. However, even at first sight it is clear that in many ways – and I cannot help but feel in the most fundamental ways – our market resembled more an archaic than a modern market.

When comparing the economic and sociological perspective on human behaviour, James Coleman (1988) shows that sociologists understand it above all as the outcome of socialisation and focus on explaining on how it is shaped, constrained and directed by its

monopoly of legitimate violence, political action proper can be exercised only by the effect of officialization and thus presupposes the competence (in the sense of a capacity socially recognized in a public authority) required in order to manipulate the collective definition of the situation in such a way as to bring it closer to the official definition of the situation and thereby to win the means of mobilizing the largest possible group, the opposite strategy tending to reduce the same situation to a merely private affair. To possess the capital of authority necessary to impose a definition of the situation, especially in the moments of crisis when the collective judgement falters, is to be able to mobilize the group by solemnizing, officializing, and thus uiniversalizing a private incident... It is also to be able to demobilize it, by disowning the person directly concerned, who, failing to identify his particular interest with the 'general interest', is reduced to the status of a mere individual, condemned to appear unreasonable in seeking to impose his private reason – idiotes in Greek and amahbul in Kabyle... It is natural that politics should be the privileged arena for the dialectic of the official and the useful: in their efforts to draw the group's delegation upon themselves and withdraw it from their rivals, the agents in competition for political power are limited to ritual strategies and strategic rituals, products of the collectivizing of private interests and the symbolic appropriation of official interests." [Bourdieu 1977: 41] social context. The weakness of their position resides in the fact that they fail to answer the question of what the basic impulse is, i.e. the engine, the driving force of such behaviour. This can lead to a situation in which it appears that humans are acting merely on the basis of impulses received from their surroundings, i.e. they are merely reacting.

Economists offer the following explanation. In the background of all human behaviour is an endeavour to maximise the benefit of the actor themselves, or to maximise the benefit of their group or organisation (and by extension their own), in which case we use the term *corporate utility*. On the other hand, the weakness of many economic theories is that they often gloss over the fact that this behaviour always takes place within the context of social norms, i.e. social networks of mutual trust or mistrust in the environment of social organisations and institutions, which are able to modify it substantially. Some social norms and pressures may cause an individual to act against the maximisation of their own benefit.

However, this objection affects only a limited segment of human behaviour. It is clear even to the most ardent social determinist that a person under the pressure of social norms renounces their own benefit with great reluctance, comports themself in this way only temporarily, and seeks to organise things in such a way that they return to the maximisation of individual rewards as soon as possible.

In the original formulation of the objectives of the new social order, the maximisation of individual rewards was more or less to be sacrificed in favour of the common weal. This objective was built on the premise that the "national interest" was syncretic, and that individual interests in the maximisation of benefit would not only be amassed, but saved and accrue interest. This in turn would lead to a "continuous rise in the standard of living of all people", as the vision of the public weal eventually materialised.

However, in order to be able to amass individual interests in this way, it was necessary to assume their commonality or uniformity.

Conflicting interests cannot be combined, but are mutually para-
lysed and cancel each other out. In order to maintain the assumption
of commonality, those whose interests were incompatible with the
new system (for instance, because they had lost all of their assets
with its arrival) had to be excluded from the notional *corpus* that
was supposed to participate in monitored *corporate utility*, for which
the common good was intended.

Everyone was to participate in it, with the exception of some who
did not deserve to. From the very start, the principle of exclusion or
expulsion was built into the logic of the system.[41] It was originally
conceived of as temporary, and after an initial period of consolida-
tion, was to be abandoned. However, as time passed, it became clear
that there was not enough room to implement the original plan to
build a classless society, and the basis of the common good both
clearly and covertly contracted step by step. After the capitalists had
been excluded, it was the turn of their children, while the shadow of
inherited sin extended ad infinitum, as the families of the establishment closed themselves into an ever more exclusive group. The time
for recruitment into the Communist Party and the Czechoslovak
Socialist Youth Union (ČSM) was over, and it was no longer the
case that "anyone can join".[42] On the contrary, a regular cycle of vetting and purging began. The sources from which the common good
was drawn were not growing as fast as anticipated, and eventually stopped growing altogether. They began to contract. The system
was caught in a negative feedback loop: with every newly excluded

---

41 An analysis of the mechanisms of exclusion in Czechoslovak society is offered by Petrusek
[1988].
42 This relative "openness" was how Vaculík described the difference between the capitalist and
socialist ruling class back in 1967 in a speech delivered at the 4th Congress of Czech Writers. He
was shown the errors of his ways very simply. He was expelled from the party and dismissed from
his employment, above all because his speech implied the attitude of "not minding the fact that
he was on the side of the exploiters." Even then, demand outstripped supply and elite power had
already sealed itself off hermetically so as to prevent the crumbling of the inheritance for its next
generation. This need, too, lay behind the call for fraternal assistance.

person, loyalty was lost (along with the loyalty of their family), and with a contracting base of loyalty, namely, a willingness to sacrifice the maximisation of one's own profit to the common good, it became necessary to exclude more and more from the common good, since the sources were insufficient. And with every newly excluded person, loyalty was lost, and so on...[43]

The shock of the 1968 invasion now laid bare for all to see the true nature of the "common good" of socialist society, while the subsequent purges sharply defined the corpus of those who, owing to the external higher power of empire, legitimised themselves as entitled beneficiaries of corporate utility. The concept of universal solidarity collapsed once and for all in the social consciousness. What might have originally been a voluntary contribution to the common good was inverted, and now became the harsh exploitation of the majority by the minority. The exclusionary principle that had divided society into "us" and "them" continued for so long that it turned into a paradox. It began with the exclusion of a small group of enemies, whose numbers continued to rise until there were so few friends that they found themselves excluded: the regime found itself besieged from all sides. A stake in the fence[44].

---

43 The entire process can be viewed as a particular example of a general mechanism. In *Tristes Tropiques*, Lévi-Strauss observes that in traditional societies, where the density of population exceeded the capacity of resources (he was prompted to make this observation by the deltas of the great rivers of Asia), mass exclusion was the outcome. An entire category of people was in principle denied their humanity, excluded from the community, and the settlement thinned out: the untouchables did not count, only those who remained were entitled to the resources. In this regard, 20th century Europe, which spawned Nazism and concentration camps, gives us pause for thought. In this country it was first the Jews. Then the Sudeten Germans, then the kulaks [wealthier, landowning peasants: t/n] and capitalists, and in the wake of 1968 the revisionists. Yet nothing was ever enough. The slogan expel! hangs in the air so thickly you could cut it with a knife. And now we'll begin the vetting process [known as lustration: t/n]. These people had no clue as to the depths from which this arose from within them.

44 The oft quoted phrase "a stake in the fence" (*kůl v plotě*), meaning to be completely alone in the world, was uttered by First Secretary of the Communist Party Miloš Jakeš in a rambling speech delivered to communist functionaries in the summer of 1989: t/n.

The idea of the common good as a reward for renouncing the maximisation of individual profit had collapsed. This was not simply due to the emergence of a new class barrier. It collapsed mainly because basic social capital, i.e. the mutual trust without which the renunciation of personal profit in favour of the common weal would be absurd, had run out. It had been completely consumed. In the end no one dared trust anyone and the pursuit of the common weal was perhaps only possible on the lowest level, that of the common interests of one's own and no one else's family.

And thus we find ourselves, having described a great arc, back with family reasons in the background of the social change being tracked.

Creeping reprivatisation on the level of big capital was, in its way, even more successful than covert reprivatisation on a lower level. Given the abstract and depersonalised character of large-scale ownership, and because in all societies the space in which the jostling for position, power and profit takes place in the sphere of large capital is socially far more closed and opaque than the space of a small enterprise, which is in direct contact with its customer, the extent of the reprivatisation of big capital in Czechoslovakia was almost completely concealed. Two facts were crucial when it came to blurring the contours of the genuine state of affairs: the non-monetary nature of ownership relations (large assets could neither be bought nor sold: true, they could be acquired and lost, but quite how was a carefully guarded secret); and the total dominance of the public semantic space already referred to, which used conceptual engineering to gloss over the social mechanisms of coercion, domination and exploitation. Right up until the very end (and even to this day), common sense had to rub its eyes in disbelief, since it was perfectly clear that large assets had once again found their way into the hands of a small group of people, the identity of many of whom was abundantly clear. Common sense knew it was being taken for a ride. It also saw how large assets were quietly passing from fathers to sons by means of the mechanism of "class criteria", and it knew that large owners were recorded in the nomenklatura more carefully than in the trade register. And yet: *after all, it belongs to the state!* (The idea that these assets belonged to "all the people" caused great merriment, since it was an assertion that was contradicted by everyday experience...)

Doubts naturally arose as to whether some of these people, by acting so clearly in their own rather than the state (collective) interest, had not fallen foul of the law. Sometimes they had, sometimes not: they did not even have to act outside the law, since it was they who formulated the law and oversaw compliance therewith. However, they, too, were held captive by the system. They could use only systemically legitimate means and issue only laws corresponding to the system. As the character of these means and the wording of these laws increasingly came into conflict with their interests, they, too, began to harbour doubts regarding the reasonableness of the system.

Inasmuch as the breakdown in mutual trust to the level of individual families was unpleasant, albeit manageable for those at the bottom, it had devastating consequences for the ruling class.[45]

Even in a modern economy based on contract law rather than on the state and possessing institutionalised apparatuses for the control of obligations and sanctions for non-compliance, a certain degree of mutual trust is indispensible, since protecting against all possible threats and covering all eventualities would be unimaginably costly: we all to an extent rely on mutual comprehension and trust.

---

[45] It was of course this new class that sought to destroy the trust between subjects in order to control them. As Hannah Arendt (1958) convincingly demonstrates, if a totalitarian system is to achieve the desired manipulation of the masses, it must atomise individual members, and the best way of achieving this end is by fomenting mutual distrust. However, this becomes an attempt to square the circle: to foment distrust in society restricted to those being controlled, while maintaining complete trust between those doing the controlling. Mistrust does not spread like AIDS, through direct contact, but more like a cold, through simply being present in an environment. Prostitutes, however, are always the first to catch both.

The situation is somewhat different in a system that enters into no written contracts pertaining to fundamental matters. Agreement in this case is not guaranteed by an external coercive apparatus independent of the contracting parties. Instead, the agreement may only be enforced by mobilising sufficient support and legitimised only through symbolic consent. Trust is crucial.

The basic requisite for being appointed director of any institution, be it an industrial enterprise or the Academy of Fine Arts, was that the person in question be a *trustworthy comrade*. This applied to the Communist Party itself, notwithstanding its ritualised voting process. If someone's name was put forward, there was no option but to vote for them since they clearly enjoyed the trust of another comrade. There was nothing to prevent one from raising one's hand against, no automatic sanctions. However, one simply *lost trust*. And trust was such a precious asset that voting tended to be unanimous...

In a detailed analysis of social capital, Coleman (1988: 101) identifies the following basic elements: obligations, justified expectations, norms and structures. Within this system trust then creates an environment, the level of which is crucial to the functioning of the other elements. Granovetter (1985) even reproaches economists for a functional aberration that prevents them from grasping that the character of *all economic behaviour* is fundamentally influenced (he uses the term embedded) by the level of confidence in the environment in which it takes place.

As the level of trust in our social environment fell, so too did the circle shrink of those to whom the *corporate utility* principle, the common good, applied. This process was interlinked internally: it seemed that mutual trust could be more easily maintained within a smaller group. The party was reduced in size by means of mass expulsions and was divided into a healthy core, i.e. the internal, genuine party, and marginal members. Finally, when even within the inner core of the party the level of trust and solidarity fell beneath the necessary minimum, this process of division was applied on the level of clienteles, family clans and individual families.

However, once individual families of the establishment began to act more or less off their own bat, each seeking merely to maximise their own profit, it became increasingly clear that the archaic system, in which profit was taboo, ownership obscured, and spheres of social life undifferentiated, was no longer able to fulfil its basic function, namely the indiscernible exploitation and reproduction of given structures of domination.

In the absence of solidarity it was deemed more and more urgent that the share of individual families in corporately managed assets should be defined more strictly and unambiguously. Individual clans sought to expand their sphere of influence. Each wanted to be the head honcho, since the maximisation of their profit and the welfare of their family depended on it. This aim could only be achieved at the expense of other comrades. However, this conflict of interests lacked an independent authority to which appeals could be submitted. Disputes were decided on by what was sometimes referred to as the Mother Party, with no trial, defence or prosecutor, with no minutes taken, no written code or archived judgement, and with no appeal process in place. An individual would be transferred from a position in the economy to the apparat, from the apparat to the state administration, thence to what were known as the "forces" (*složky*), i.e. the institutions of symbolic and direct coercion. Since each person carried with them their accumulated social capital, i.e. their obligations and legitimate expectations, during each such transfer, the entire system fused into one whole, like a ball of plastic string exposed to heat. No matter how tightly bound and impossible to untangle the ball of string had been to begin with, by the end there was nothing left to untangle. However, inside the conflicts of interest grew, the stresses intensified, greed increased, and resources dwindled.

Under such conditions it is only natural that *within the ruling class*, the group of those who perceived the necessity of fundamental change to the system of domination expanded dynamically. We must not be misled by the easy prejudice that equates members of the nomenklatura with workers of the Party apparat. However difficult it may be to believe, there were in their ranks individuals with a knowledge of history and an internationalist outlook. These included directors of the Regional Institutes of National Health and cultivated doctors, directors of research institutes with genuinely international reputations and contacts, and above all many managers of commercial, financial and manufacturing organisations whose work inevitably brought them into contact with a "competing" system and who had no choice but to compare their status, options and profits with colleagues on the other side. The comparison was truly soul destroying.

The distaste that the Czech intellectual feels for the highest levels of management, whether administrative or economic (not to mention political), and their links to the vassals of imperial power, must not blind us to the fact that many of these managers regarded these links as an unpleasant but unavoidable part of the successful exercise of their profession, and that among their ranks were many capable and efficient individuals. With the possible exception of East Germany (comparisons with which were made difficult by the tacit support of Big Brother [Russia: t/n]), Czechoslovakia boasted the most productive economy of the Eastern bloc.[46] Up until the end of the 1960s, the country's standard of living kept pace with that of Austria and Finland, and even exceeded that of the more traditionally based societies of Western Europe such as Spain and Portugal, not to speak of Turkey. Attempts to explain this by appealing to the "legacy of the democratic past" are vague, and the reputation enjoyed by the Czechs, at least among themselves, for "golden

---

46 Though they operated within the same socialist economy as other COMECON countries, the Czechs and Slovaks were the only ones to ensure that cars were freely available on the market at a reasonable price. They also created the most comprehensive telephone network.

hands" is misleading: in a modern economy wealth is not generated by hands, but heads.

However, the empire did not favour the "clever Czech heads"[47] of its outlying provinces. The Communist Party organised regular inspections as part of the system of tightening up central power through instilling in people a fear of losing their jobs. The people who failed these inspections tended to be independent thinkers and entrepreneurial, dynamic individuals with aspirations that transcended everyday routine. On the contrary, the people promoted by the Party to managerial positions were dull, cautious and lacking in vision: in a word, stupid. As Jiří Kroha, an architect with a penetrating social intelligence (and great – how can I put it? – social flexibility), once said to me of someone else: "He was selected because he is stupid enough to offer the security of loyalty: he hasn't got the brains to organise an act of treachery."

Using the same yardsticks, these stupid people then chose as their subordinates people even stupider than they. The pyramids of stupidity grew. On the fifth rung down the ladder of subordination the demand for simple-mindedness was so high that sufficiently stupid candidates were difficult to find. This in turn prompted complaints that supplies had dried up, for the population at large seemed overall simply too intelligent. The result was that the cleverest established a niche for themselves at the very bottom of the pile, since they were able to feign indolence. They then rose inexorably up the hierarchy, and after a while there was nothing for it but to organise a new round of lustration.

The vetting that took place in the 1970s put the finishing touches to the entire process. Decent people refused to cooperate, and so it was not the second rung but the fifth that triumphed. This caused the Czechoslovak economy to lag behind the competition, and in

---

47 The adage in full reads: *Zlaté české ručičky a chytré české hlavičky* or "Golden Czech hands and clever Czech heads": t/n.

many sectors we basically gave up. However, we were dependent on the world economy, and ensuring that inconvenient ideas remained beyond the borders of the state, even one surrounded by barbed wire, is unrealistic within the framework of the contemporary global electronic village.[48] Twenty years is a long time, and the old process repeated. In the late 1980s, that element of the ruling class that was intrinsically tied to its archaic nature was convulsed by a contradiction that proved to be intractable. On the one hand, it felt its contracting base to be at threat in light of its encirclement by a population it now had little to offer and that was basically doing its own thing: on the other hand, it was terrified that even within its fortifications, the majority of its defenders were already sympathetic to the besiegers. More lustration was called for! Too many wise guys who could not be trusted had sneaked back into the citadel...

At first glance, the main problem seemed to be the artists, many of whom, though belonging to the nomenklatura and very much part of the system, were losing their fear and beginning to display signs of disobedience. Their expulsion would not have been a problem had they not reflected the opinions of broad circles of the technical, scientific, administrative and humanist intelligentsia, without which a modern society cannot be governed. Many of these, who had been the lifeblood of the new regime twenty years earlier, now stepped enthusiastically or shamefacedly into still warm shoes in hierarchies thinned out by the great generational purge, and, after two decades enduring the futility of an outdated system, arrived at the same place as their predecessors, intellectually speaking, but now furnished with the memory of the latters' experience: exchanging the face of this regime for a human one means modifying its very essence.

---

48 Rabušic [1990] regards this to be one of the three basic causes of the inevitable collapse of the old system.

However, many regarded the archaic way of exercising power as fundamentally flawed from the very start. They regarded it as foreign to our culture, as barbaric and forcibly imported. They were only reconciled to it because nothing else was conceivable.

They waited. And the empire that had imposed the system on us slowly lost its strength until the time came when the question of fundamental reform could no longer be ignored. They had not waited in vain.

No one will ever provide empirical proof of how many of those that the party considered its most loyal foot soldiers were, by the end of the 1980s, secretly prepared to betray the old system. If we once again recall that the nomenklatura contained not only the ruling element of the coercive system of brutal, symbolic domination, but also the large, executive elite of the administrative, economic and educational sectors, intuition would tell us it was a majority.

One thing is for sure: there is no point in relying on what they say today. These days almost everyone is a reformist in hindsight. It's just that their voice was ignored... But this is in many ways merely a projection onto the past of the opinions of the present, the wisdom of generals after losing the fight: if only the monarch had listened to us... However, we will never know for sure, not even if we could ask people prior to the collapse of the establishment. Not just because we would not receive an honest answer. Change was taking place at snail's pace, at low levels of mutual trust and without articulation, so that many an important figure of the old regime themselves did not know how deeply they were convinced of the need to kickstart capitalism in Czechoslovakia. The dismantling of the old system was not achieved through natural wastage of the loyal cadre, but because the level of scepticism rose even amongst those faithful to the regime, invisibly and at a different tempo in the case of each individual, with the sole exception of those who suspected that there would be no room for them in a different system. As regards those who were inseparably associated with the archaic form of the system, there was a sense of increasing anxiety and menace that, transformed into aggression, accelerated developments.

And so when evaluating the overall extent of the dissolution of loyalty to the old system in our establishment, the most reliable tool is the old Marxist concept of group or class interest, which may or may not be conscious. The only difference lies in whether we speak of class "in itself" or class "for itself". As a class in itself, our "new class", especially its elite in the economic as well as the professional-managerial, scholarly, humanities and educational spheres, was unequivocally in favour of an underlying change of relations, though its members may have been unaware of the fact.

Objective interest, whether knowingly or not, focused the minds of a substantial part of the new class on objectives we can summarise in a few points. Unconsciously or consciously, radically or conservatively, with a lightness or heaviness of heart, they sought a way to transform the current system into a more modern, economically and socially effective system, while holding on to everything their family had been able to accumulate thus far. A system in which "relations of dominance take on the lustre and permanence of objects and are beyond the reach of individual consciousness and power", a system in which the "permanence and cumulativeness of material and symbolic acquisitions which can exist without their holders having to renew them by deliberate actions", and where "dominance does not have to be realised in a direct, personal way." Such a system was certainly what they wished for their children, and they did not have to invent it – it was there in front of their eyes, or, as we say in this country, just "over the hill" (*za kopečky*)[49]. However, reconfiguring an entire country was more difficult and riskier than slipping quietly through the Iron Curtain on an individual basis. This was not an option for the elites (even though of the younger generation the sons of the nomenklatura were over represented in emigration figures

---

49 *Za kopečky*, an idiom used in relation to emigration: t/n.

during the final years), since they would be unable to take all of their assets, property and status with them. In short, they needed to introduce a more modern system of dominance and exploitation to this country.

In order to achieve that aim, several systemic changes had to be made. Though no one at the time would have enumerated them as follows, for the needs of our analysis we can categorise them under seven points. Whether they were aware of the fact or not, the elite needed to take the following steps.

1. **They needed to rid themselves of their dependency on social capital** and convert their assets into economic capital. This point is crucial and the other six all derive from it. The pressure for this was exerted mainly by the youngest generation of the new class, the children of the establishment rulers. It was their side of the family interest, for it was this change that facilitated the transfer of the real base of dominance to future generations: to an extent it was the condition thereof.

Social capital is hardly the foundation on which dynasties are built: some form of treasure must be in the chest even with the full legitimacy of succession. And this was lacking in the communist system. It was its neuralgic point.[50] Social capital has a fundamental disadvantage against economic capital, in that it is contextually bound, while the beautiful thing about money is that it is contextually entirely neutral. Dodgy acquaintances cannot be deposited in a bank and then used in a different context: dirty money can. (The economy does not recognise the term dirty money. It cannot afford to. It would kill the market if it were necessary to corroborate the origin of cash during every payment.) This is also the reason why social capital as a good is extremely fragile and perishable. Its

---

50 As we know from history, on the top level this led to frightful pogroms of entire clans during the handover of power.

registration is difficult and it can only be reliably stored in the mind of its owner,[51] which in this respect no computer can replace. It cannot be moved around, and every change of constellation in the social environment necessitates a laborious and costly rearrangement of the network, an activity that our powers had to engage in regularly with all the patience of Brittany fishermen, but without their serene equanimity, because for them an error did not involve the loss of a few fish, but their entire existence. When the son of a government minister saw how small a stumble on his father's part it took for him to become the son of a nobody overnight (at best: at worst, then the son of a class enemy and pariah of the highest order), and when the grandson of a regional chief saw how quickly the nimbus of inviolability that had until then surrounded him dissipated because the power of the patriarch had disappeared on the day he retired – can we be surprised that they demanded a different way of insuring their future existence?

However, in addition to thinking of the future, attention gradually turned to the immediate present. As Szelenyi (1990) convincingly showed, in Eastern-bloc countries two stratification pyramids gradually formed. The first was the establishment pyramid, backed by social capital, and the second the economic pyramid, backed by private economic capital, albeit modest to begin with. These two pyramids intersected, just as both forms of capital are simply two sides of one and same coin in terms of power. However, at their tips they were completely independent. Szelenyi points to Hungary, where this phenomenon was most apparent, and shows that the successful families of the second market eventually acquired the self-confidence of the emancipated elite and were not ashamed to indulge in conspicuous

---

51 In this respect it is worth nothing the observation made by the development anthropologists Tiger and Fox: "We kept both our primate inheritances, body and group, but we found a way of expanding our societies, though our bodies remained substantially the same – except for our heads, which we filled with brain tissue, in good part to keep track of our extended web of people and ideas about people." (Tiger and Fox 1971: 36)

consumption. In terms of the prestige and appeal of their position, they competed successfully with families at the peak of the pyramid of official power. In Czechoslovak society, too, the feeling spread that, while the elite of the second economy could destroy the regime, the elite of the regime could not destroy the second economy.

For younger generations this meant that, while a successful black marketeer[52] could afford to present the lady of his life a white Mercedes as a status symbol, the son of a government minister could do no such thing, though he might be competing for the favours of the same lady. The minister's son did not have the proper currency, and, even if by chance he did, he was not in a position to demonstrate the fact by spending it: this would put his father's position at risk, since it would undermine the capital on which the latter depended. This could sometimes be quite humiliating, and so depending on the situation the youngest generation reached the conclusion that, though social status was a wonderful thing, it needed to be backed by something more secure than merely the intertwining of old obligations, reciprocated favours, and mutual *kompromat*. For instance, by a legitimate account in a reliable bank.

Slowly but surely, a third reason why it was essential to change the basic form of capital became clear to the elite. One outcome of the ongoing debate over the concept of social network in Anglo-Saxon sociology (cf. for instance Ben-Porath 1980, Granovetter 1985, Wellman and Berkowitz 1988 and the main articles in the *American Journal of Sociology* 96) was clarification of the conceptual difference between strong ties and weak ties in the social fabric of a society. In simple terms, strong ties are those into which a person is born or within which they are bound by parentage or contract (e.g. employment), while weak ties are less determinative and arise more or less

---

52 *Vekslák*, someone involved in the illegal purchase and sale of foreign currencies and so-called *bony*, i.e. vouchers that could be exchanged for foreign and deluxe goods in branches of Tuzex, a series of state-run shops: t/n.

spontaneously, selectively and pragmatically. I have previously shown how even the social networks of family clans must be supplemented with persons unrelated by blood, a situation already pertaining in the Middle Ages in the concept of clientship (Možný 1982). However, traditional societies were reliant more on strong, namely kinship, relations. The archaic goodwill economy found in these a kind of objective security, and its resuscitation in Central Europe, along with the amalgam of tradition and modernity already described, returned to these relations in the form of a carefully concealed but egregious nepotism. However, while traditional societies could rely on (fairly) strong kinship relations, modern societies cannot, for two reasons. Firstly, they are more complex: each individual's network of action is considerably wider than even the most broadly conceived family, including second-generation cousins. And secondly, in modern societies the relatives in a network decrease as the number of children in a family declines and spatial mobility increases. If we add to this the instability of the modern family, the chaos that multiple marriages wreak and the hostility that reigns between original partners, we see that this is by no means a strong fabric forming the social network. Nepotism in an unstable family with an only child is like a yacht trying to cross an ocean over which jet planes fly: Thor Heyerdahl showed that it can be done.

All of which meant there was no alternative but to attempt the following:

2. **The restoration of the institution of private ownership.** We have shown how, even in the sphere of large ownership (of the means of production), a form of concealed reprivatisation took place and the disintegration of corporate utility into that of individual clans and families. However, it was in the interest of the ruling oligarchy to render property relations transparent so that they could be controlled. The original advantage of opacity, namely, that it protected the class of de facto owners against outside control, gradually proved

less important than the impossibility of mutual control within an ownership group.[53] Given internal relations within the elite, the following became increasingly necessary:

3. **The dissolution of the conglomerate of the economic, administrative, political and coercive sectors** so that they could operate as mutually independent and self-governing institutions and guarantee legitimised ownership relations. Again, an extremely risky operation, but increasingly unavoidable. Herein resides Gorbachev's squaring of the circle. The leading role of the party: can't live with it, can't live without it.

And so it became necessary:

4. **To change the method of control by moving from symbolic dominance and brute force to a subtler economic dominance.** It was clear that only the legitimisation of greed as the driver of economic growth and the goal of all the work of economic organisations would allow for their reorganisation oriented openly on the maximisation of profit, and that only this would in turn lead to an increase in productivity to a level comparable with advanced economies. This would then allow the elite:

5. **To rationalise the exercise of power** by getting rid of the vast apparatuses of the state police and propaganda, ranging from undercover employees of the ministry of the interior to teachers of scientific atheism, i.e. people who had an existential interest in the continuation of the archaic system, since within modern systems they

---

53 However, the reformers did not want to give up the advantages of opacity. In order to have their cake and eat it, they considered a "plurality of forms of ownerships" with private property, to begin with squeezed into the small economy, and large ownership remaining opaque in quasi-cooperative enterprises that would in reality be owned as Slušovice is owned by Čuba [from 1963 to 1990, František Čuba was CEO of JZD Slušovice – Jednotné zemědělské družstvo meaning collective farm: t/n]. Converting later cooperative shares into stock and thus smoothly establishing private ownership seemed like a relatively viable plan.

would become completely surplus to requirements. There were, of course, numerous family ties and old commitments, though overall the economic and professional-managerial elite felt more and more strongly that if the previous five points were not realised, the idea of a gradual eradication or, on the contrary, cultivation of this element, which was characterised by strong internal cohesion and suspicion verging on paranoia, was unrealistic. As the new class settled down, it felt more and more strongly that though these satraps of power were keeping it in the driving seat, they were also compromising it to an unacceptable degree. As long as it kept them in its ranks, it would not be possible:

6. **To regain its dominant status with the lustre** granted it by the objectivisation of social capital in modern institutions. Personal dignity is a social value that, in my opinion, sociology as a category of social analysis fails to appreciate. Many of the powerful paid for their position through a loss of dignity, not only in the eyes of the public, but in their own eyes and those of their children. It was a burden that, when they took it upon themselves, seemed insignificant, but the weight of which, over time, became so heavy that many found it unbearable.[54]

One or more of these six points proved more or less unacceptable to this or that element of the new class, and the final years were marked by the search for a tolerable combination. However, it became increasingly clear that only if they accepted all as elements of

---

54 Bourdieu (1977) cites noble titles, property rights and academic qualifications as an example of institutions that lend lustre and permanence to domination. The first two institutions were abolished by the revolution so ostentatiously that their re-introduction seemed out of the question. Many attempted it with academic titles, though without much success. For instance, Doc. Ing. RSDr. Antonín Kapek, CSc, who fell from the tip of the pyramid of the Prague party apparat in the mid-1980s, found few handholds in the letters surrounding his name. However, sometimes such a collection of letters offered a measure of consolation in the event of forced departure from places of genuine power in the apparat.

a single logical system would they achieve the most desirable goal, namely:

7. **Their own self-reproducibility**. It was an either/or situation. No intermediate state was possible, in the same way that it is not possible to be partly pregnant:

> "On the one side there are social relations which, not containing within themselves the principle of their own reproduction, must be kept up through nothing less than a process of continuous creation; on the other side, a social world which, containing within itself the principle of its own continuation, frees agents from the endless work of creating or restoring social relations." (Bourdieu 1977: 189)

This liberation has profound consequences in respect of reflections upon the social. As Bourdieu points out, in order for the social sciences to come into existence, it was first necessary to jettison the notion that the social order was maintained by the intentions, purposeful actions and will of individuals. Only in a world of self-sustaining institutions did the limits of the "sovereign will" of the individual and its relative insignificance in the organisation of the social world become clear. Hobbes, as Durkheim pointed out, proceeded from the premise that it was "an act of will which gives rise to social order and an act of will, that is constantly renewed, which maintains it." (Durkheim 1953)[55]. And we can go even further, to the very notion of the Cartesian universe, which cannot exist without the relentless participation of God, an idea that Leibnitz had already criticised in the conception of a God condemned to move the world "as a carpenter moves his axe or as a miller drives his millstone by directing water towards the wheel".

---

55 Quoted from Lukes, Steven: *Emile Durkheim: His Life and Work.* Stanford: Stanford University Press, 1973, 287.

We have every reason to believe that the break with this vision, which is the basis of scientific thought, could not have taken place until such objective mechanisms as the self-regulating market – which, as Polanyi shows, incorporates determinism as a prerequisite within itself (Cf. Polanyi 1968 and Bourdieu 1977) – were constituted in reality.[56]

At many points in my reasoning the reader might begin to suspect that I was actually attempting to demonstrate the same thing as the worst tabloid press, namely, that what we call the "Velvet Revolution" was simply a grandiose scam aimed at dazzling the foolish, and that those who curated it achieved their ends and once again have the reins of power firmly in their grip. Not at all. I hope that no one believes I could have anything to do with such an interpretation.

Solid historiography refutes such a view, which implies a conspiratorial conception of history as the outcome of secret alliances, both factually and methodically. Norbert Wiener (1963) once used the expression "Machiavellian conception of history", though this is to do Machiavelli a disservice. It is a far older form of thinking, grounded in the archaic way of organising society. Those who thus defend the "results of their revolutionary determination" against the "dark forces of the old regime" would be surprised at the extent to which their own thinking is in the power of dark forces – of traditional reasoning. I am attempting to make the opposite point: that the revolution took place in Czechoslovakia not ultimately on the basis of a conspiracy or plan, whether one believes the movers of history were the Chartists (and the large number of people who suddenly

---

56 From this point of view, Stalin's declared prolongation of the season for "intensification of the class struggle" indefinitely was not merely a tactical justification for repression, show trials and purges. It was an unconscious admission that the archaic system did not contain within itself the principle of its own continuity, as he had originally believed. It was an admission that, if the system was to sustain itself, it would have to be renewed through the perpetual deployment of violence. It was also of course an expression of Stalin's illusion that his people would be sufficiently resilient. Which they were – but only until his death, after which the entire empire began to crumble.

remembered they had always agreed with them but had kept the fact secret for obvious reasons), or some mysterious clique in the background of the nomenklatura that still pulls the strings. Instead, I am arguing that the revolution took place as the realisation of a vector of the intersecting, largely long-term interests of diverse individuals and entire social groups, interests which not even they themselves were aware of that had consequences that no one had intended.

It goes without saying that conscious intentions and Machiavellian conspiracies existed here and still do. But they failed. Everyone experienced (and is still experiencing) something different to what they had anticipated. The intentions of the old Brezhnevian class, which had hoped to render perestroika a cosmetic operation that would leave everything unchanged (especially their own class) came to naught, as did the plans of pretenders to the throne who wanted by means of the Trojan horse of perestroika to transfer their social capital unscathed into a new, more modernised "market socialism". And this is not to speak of the conspiracy of those who wished to remain in the background and are at present negotiating as to whether they will be investigated in freedom... Then there were the plans of the old regime's opponents, who looked forward to being free to pursue a kind of "apolitical politics" unencumbered by the outdated concept of a political party, but rather on the basis of a movement that would maintain the consensus created by resistance... Nada. And what about the old dream that society would finally become truly fair, without dominance and exploitation... Should I carry on? Now we have what we wanted, it looks a hell of lot different to what we imagined.

As indeed it will. As much as I like the idea that it is the old elite that will most pay for the changes in circumstances, I'm afraid that, as a sociologist, I have to accept that things are more complex. I simply cannot share the illusion – in essence not dissimilar to a New Year resolution to do things differently "from tomorrow on" – that after the fall of the communist regime we simply replace everyone who played a part in perpetuating its existence. Not even the plebeian notion that it will not be "us" who are got rid of (the people cannot be replaced), but "them", the "other families", wholly and mercilessly. Even if all the Chartists abandoned their jobs as translators, priests, journalists, philosophers and dramatists, the 1,864 signatories of Charta 77 are not up to the job – and a substantial majority of them will stay in their own lane. And the situation will be no better if we add the 39,000 signatories of the *Několik vět* petition[57] and their families. In short, even if we add everyone who sincerely hated the old system, but simply did not consider it meaningful or reasonable in their position to sign some manifesto or other, we're back where we started.

And so we must expect substantial numbers of the old administrative and economic elites to use their cultural capital (since the hands-on experience they have of how the state and economy function will not be taken away from them without taking away whatever they possess in the way of talent, dedication and managerial skill) and social capital to traverse the narrow pass of social change. Or at least in numbers more significant that we would like to see from the perspective of historical justice. There has understandably been significant movement in this class, and this will continue. The social change we are speaking of freed up the space for talented and capable people who had up till then been held in secondary or completely subordinate positions by the exclusivity of the communist bosses' club and the system of cadre branding. Space is opening up for a younger, aspiring generation that had sufficient patience and intelligence not to become part of the old cadre. Many have fled and will continue to flee who were associated with the old system of domination. Prominent agents of the police and symbolic coercive power have already lost their livelihood. The social capital they

---

57 A Few Sentences, a list of demands compiled by Charta 77 and published on 29 June 1989: t/n.

enjoyed in the old networks was contextually bound and suffered dramatic devaluation. They will find a certain support in the established administrative and economic elite, though this is already taken up with its own survival. A long-term struggle, crucial from the point of view of the success of systemic change, has begun over the restructuring and downsizing of the state administration. There is a real concern that only the collapse of entire sectors (education, health, public safety, the maintenance and development of physical infrastructure from drainage to communications, welfare covering the unsuccessful and unadaptable...) on a local and even partially central level will lead, via new political mechanisms, to the replacement of incompetent employees and to organisational change. In the economy, the path to the replacement of people and systemic changes of large ownership will be no less lengthy and difficult, perhaps with the difference that in this sector it is possible (indeed inevitable) to ensure that the collapse of a company (bankruptcy) is a permanent element of operations. But it will keep hitting stiff resistance, all the more difficult to overcome, since the management of any old structure will receive the support of its employees, whilst populist promises of "ensuring security" will be difficult to counter... In the sphere of the state and municipal authorities, nepotistic practices and work with social capital will display wonderful tenacity everywhere. Sociological studies from Greece, Portugal and Spain demonstrate its durability. It took Italy more than twenty years to get rid of these practices, and to this day some believe that it would be more productive to split Lo Stivale ("The Boot") in two and relieve themselves of the socially non-modern south... Hard times lie ahead.

However, the final outcome will not be guaranteed by employee churn, but by systemic change. Let us hope that this will involve the impartial selection of new personnel. Like the mills of the gods, it is a process that will grind slowly.

It is only to be expected that we will be impatient. However, we will gain nothing by returning to the old illusions. We cannot avoid confronting the fact that this was not a social change that will abolish domination and exploitation for good, but a change that is productive, that cultivates and gradually creates a political and economic space for a higher level of human dignity. We cannot ask for more. As Dahrendorf says:

> "In practice it is difficult to think of human association without an element of domination. Where there is society there is power. Certain authors… dream of an association freed of all elements of domination. Theirs is the language which appeals in revolutionary moments of elation. It has little use at other times, except to prepare people for unusual days which cannot last." (1988: 26)

Even worse, we will be saying goodbye to the hope that the Velvet Revolution will finally sweep into the dustbin of history those who drank our blood for years: all of them, from top to bottom. But only a certain segment of the population has such a strong desire for domination that it will sacrifice anything – comfort, friends, family life – to get its way. For others it is not worth the effort. Where such a desire is accompanied by a talent for this type of domination, which is legitimate in the best of all bad forms of government, i.e. in liberal democracy, there will no longer be anything in liberal democracy that would eliminate such individuals permanently. We can label and maintain surveillance over perhaps a few thousand people. But this then pushes back into a system that does not include within itself the principle of its own reproduction, and must be forever protected against collapse. And in any case, nothing has changed. And why should it? If a former secretary for ideology, as owner of a cheese factory, wants to expand the range of goods on offer, it is up to his competitors to step on his toes. My own interest lies in enjoying the widest selection of cheeses. Revolutionary change resides in the fact that, in the interest of its own dominance, it can no longer force me to act the fool at the Evening University of Marxism-Leninism and can no longer hit me over the head with a baton if I don't like its cheese.[58]

And that is no small gain.

---

58 It is of course to be regretted that said former secretary for ideology will have a bigger car than me. For a certain concept of the idea of justice as the philosophy of envy, this is an unacceptable outcome. I may feel sorry for those who cannot abandon this ideologised envy, but I will be against them returning to power. Already once in our lives we were so keen to ensure that no one got rich that we were all miserably poor.

Chapter Three

Now what?

Ah, but by looking to the future we are moving beyond the boundaries of this text. My aim was simply to offer some thoughts regarding the past and leave considerations of the future to the reader.

So it now remains simply to answer the third and final question: **Who were the people that poured onto the streets and filled up the squares?**

After all that I have written, the answer may be something of a damp squib: it was basically everyone. Some, it is true, were there in a professional capacity; some with the illusion that they would lead from the front; some with deeply ambivalent feelings in which fear prevailed over hope. However, the closer to the base of the social pyramid, the more strongly hope prevailed. This was because even the small owners under the spell of the "second economy" suffered from the fact that they could not "call on the state to enforce their claims".[59] Even in the case of a small rural carpenter, metalworker or plumber working in an improvised workshop or at their customers', when at last he returned from his main (official) employment, it was extremely disadvantageous that a significant number of his clients were members of his extended family clan, for whom he had to offer a "special price" depending on how closely they were related or how high were the expectations of this special relationship. He did not pay tax, true, but this also meant he kept no accounts, could not advertise for more clients, could not purchase equipment and expand his business, and could not take on apprentices and pass on the more strenuous work to them, so that in his dotage he might fall back on selling only his professional experience. He could not apply for bank loans, he was embroiled in

---

59   As Collins [1975:] writes: "The property, of course, is not the physical goods themselves, but rather a set of rights stating what some individuals can do and other individuals cannot do. Land is property not because of some metaphysical relationship between the owner and the earth, but because owners have organized their relationships to their fellows so that the owners can step on it and the nonowners cannot without the owners' permission, and owners can draw on the violence of the estate to enforce their claims."

the tangled web of the goodwill economy along with his suppliers, and he could not move house because he would be lost without his acquired contacts. His hands and feet were tied, and if he kicked the walking stick from those even more impeded than he, he acted in accordance with the rules of the system: he relied on the fact that in an archaic economy not even they "could call on the state to enforce their claims".

And so in November and December 1989, a memorable year, we all gathered in our town squares. Rhetoric again insists that we were there as The People. Here I am attempting to defend the idea that we gathered there as small (though by no means *only* small) owners. And we participated in a revolution that had already once taken place, long ago, as far back as our cultural memory reaches. As Marcel Mauss writes of the oldest attempt to create order in things that we desperately needed to have better organised: "For it is precisely the Romans and Greeks, who, perhaps, following upon the Semites of the north and west, invented the distinction between personal and real law, separated sale from gift and exchange, isolated the moral obligation and contract, and in particular, conceived the difference that exists between rites, laws, and interests. It was they who, after a veritable, great, and admirable revolution, went beyond all the outmoded morality, and this economy of the gift. It was too dependent on chance, was overexpensive and too sumptuous, burdened with consideration for people, incompatible with the development of the market, commerce, and production, and, all in all, at that time was anti-economic." (Mauss 1966: 69)

And so it is not the much proclaimed socialist utopia of economic equality and absolute social justice that is collapsing before our eyes today, but rather the quietly realised utopia of money-free domination within the context of a modern, complex society that has exhausted its possibilities and recognised and even admitted its weakness.

All thoughts regarding a "Third Way" are based on an erroneous conceptualisation of social and economic realities. The question of whether or not we should opt for a third way is poorly framed: there is no third way. In fact, we found ourselves on the third way a long time ago and now the only question is how to get off it.

The attempt to delineate its contours is now behind us. It failed. It was an attempt at a third way situated between, on the one hand, an archaic economy based on the social capital of personal power, primitively institutionalised domination and, on a market that allowed for no profit, the function of the engine of society's reproduction; and, on the other, a modern economy that embarked on its long journey through an act of discovery on the part of the ancient Greeks.

However, this means that, as a society, we are faced with changes the depth of which are hard to imagine, for all we might say that we must start from scratch.

I am afraid that more will need to be done for socialism than to find a new name for it. It seems to me that we will have to overcome its conceptualisation of the social question and attempt a radical new way of achieving its basic goal, namely, to cross the boundaries of a system where we are all *institutionally obliged* to participate in economic enterprise and to strive for constant material enrichment.

This is because the plebeian perspective of the maximisation of utility that has occupied my attention, and that from my perspective as a sociologist I must share, at least to the extent that I deem it a decisive source of the dynamic of social behaviour, is potentially open to other solutions.

However, if the search for such solutions and the associated risks are worthy of human endeavour, this is already a matter of personal value selection and not sociological reasoning. Environmentalists claim that if we do not reach the correct decision in good time, humanity has no chance. Indeed, a more sensitive ear hears that human greed, the driving force common to both the archaic and modern socialist economy (and not the feature that distinguishes one from the other, as we have been led to believe), is already occasionally scraping the bottom with its long arm.

And yet... will we ever overcome this greed?

POSTSCRIPT

Revolution is a costly step in the evolution of society. It is paid for not so much by what it destroys through its violence (which can be offset by the "velvetiness" of said revolution), but rather by virtue of the fact that it is unable to remove the old illusions *without replacing them by new ones*. These "extraordinary days that have no longue durée" will always construct a monument in history that will cast a shadow at least a generation long.

As far back as the mid-20th century, the hope was being expressed that the age of revolutions had come to an end in Europe. They had passed in a long wave from West to East and disappeared beyond the horizon of the Urals...[60] We had no choice but, albeit hesitantly or velvetly, to take up once more this outdated tool of social change. The illusions with which we have become so infected will be seen in sharp detail by our children. Before we bring this essay to an end, let us touch on one of them, which is already visible today.

This is the illusion that social capital is dispensable when it comes to running a modern society. Of course, as the backbone of great social systems, social capital has indeed become obsolete. That is precisely what this whole essay is about. But to imagine that modern society, albeit governed by other principles, can do without social capital entirely, stems from a revolutionary radicalism that knows only how to turn black into white and vice versa.

The collapse of despotic socialism in Central and Eastern Europe is widely seen as a defeat in its *economic* competition with capitalism, as a kind of macro-bankruptcy. Well ok, we went broke. But it

---

60 This wave began in the 16th century in England. At the end of the 18th century it passed through France and in the 19th century it progressed through the Springtime of Nations in Central Europe. At the beginning of the 20th century it reached Russia, where it culminated in the Great October Socialist Revolution.
After the Second World War it surged for the last time in China and thus reached the second side of the continent...

was far more about social bankruptcy than economic, even if at first glance material poverty offers itself as the main difference between us and the West. However, where our balance sheet is most unbalanced is not so much the structure and level of our economy as the structure and level of social capital.

As the economic squeeze begins, a tension rises to the surface with which the entire population struggles to maintain a minimum amount of trust in order to preserve an orderly social life. In a recent opinion poll, only 31% of Brno citizens said they regarded their fellow citizens as in general "trustworthy" or at least "quite trustworthy". When a similar question was posed in Holland, the results were 88% to 90% of respondents.[61]

Our trust deficit has several levels. It begins with a *crisis of self-belief.* Under the old system we all dreamed of what we would achieve were it not for the Bolsheviks... Well now the Bolsheviks have gone and we awaken from a nightmare in which we are failing and our old ideas are being revealed merely as self-flattering fantasies. And we have no choice, we have to realise our old projects, because we can no longer continue along the old tracks.

However, what is crucial is the *mutual trust* deficit. Here we have lost the most. After the spectre of communism gave up its circumnavigation of Europe, the younger spectre of the mafia took its place. Central and Eastern Europe are home to the highest number of Mafiosi per square kilometre. We have an apparatchik Mafia, dissident Mafia, secret police Mafia, agricultural Mafia, communist Mafia, regional Mafia, managerial Mafia... It would seem that everyone assumes that everyone else is conspiring against them, organised within a secret network, while he himself, as an honourable citizen,

---

61   This is a question regularly posed in European public opinion polls. The figures above apply to Holland between 1976 and 1985. Similar results were recorded for Britain and Luxembourg (c.f. Inglehart 1990 and Rabušic 1991).

remains to one side of this moral degeneracy and proudly bears the heavy burden of his moral rectitude.

When our children are finally in a position to be able to laugh over the problems of their parents, their mirth will probably be directed at the means by which the justified persecution complex from the period of non-freedom was transformed, at precisely the moment when fear of persecution had already lost its basis, into a new fear of being surrounded by Mafiosi. They will no doubt wonder how we learned to be so afraid.

The third level consists of a lack of trust in the authorities. Even here the difference between the situation in the Czech Republic and that in stabilised states is greater than the difference between the range of goods on offer in PRIOR [a Czech shop selling home appliances: t/n] and VROOM & DREESMANN [a Dutch chain store founded in 1887: t/n]. With the possible exception of an office where you might have a cousin, the authorities in this country are regarded not as public servants, but as dangerous sinecures for "those other families". In the eyes of the public, the local council is not run by "us", but by "them", notwithstanding the fact that "we" voted "them" into power in free and fair elections.

The fourth level of the trust deficit is the lack of a solid belief in a new form of *social institution*. The new form of the institution of ownership, state, work, law, etc., etc., has difficulty in winning full confidence in its own legitimacy. This is something that will take several generations.

However, if we lack faith in ourselves, if we do not trust each other enough, if we don't believe in our own authorities and we are uncertain regarding the new form of basic social institutions, then how can we have *confidence in our own future*? Everything would seem to suggest that here is where the fifth deficit lies.

Strangely, as regards faith in the future, the situation in the Czech Republic does not look so bleak. There is certainly a deficit. However, it is paradoxically far smaller than one might expect. Opinion polls show that a significant majority of the population has strong faith in the future. But before we get too complacent, let's not forget that this doesn't mean that people are thinking of our common future, in any sense of that word. Asked in August 1990 about his faith in the future of the Czechoslovak Federation, Jiří Suchý replied carefully that he had faith in the future of Czechs and the future of Slovaks, whatever the outcome of the Federation.

It is when projecting into the future that we encounter the sixth and deepest layer of our crisis of confidence. Our optimism is sadly of an exclusively individual character, lacking the awareness of the crucial dependence of outcomes on efficient cooperation. We have a deficit of *faith in joint action*. The idea of non-revolutionary, ongoing, patient cooperation on a long-term project on a federal, regional, municipal, professional, or neighbourly level is one we find problematic...

It is no wonder. The last battle that we Czechs won (though even then we lost the war) was probably the Battle of Dolní Věstonice in 1619[62,63]. All of the wisdom of our history teaches us that, whenever there is open confrontation, gathering in a crowd is not the best idea... We are too few to form a sufficiently large assembly. Every such gathering simply makes us a more identifiable and vulnerable target. And so in an attempt to maximise utility, the wise man will avoid the company of others, and if this is impossible, then he joins them discreetly or secretly. Which takes us back to this fascination with the Mafia: though our wise man may not join such a group himself, he assumes that others do.

---

62 Also known as the Battle of Wisternitz and fought on 5 August 1619 between a Moravian force and an Austrian army: t/n.
63 Perhaps. It is significant that the experts and historians interviewed could not agree on when the last victorious battle took place. The opinion was even voiced that one would have to look back as far as Přemysl Otakar II [Ottokar II, the Iron and Golden King, reigned as King of Bohemia from 1253 until his death in 1278: t/n].

Just as we do not overcome economic bankruptcy by abolishing the economy, but by restructuring it, so we do not deal with the problem of social capital merely by declaring it passé. Here, too, we face a complex process of transformation. We cannot yet be sure, but many indicators appear to be suggesting that on all levels – as individuals, families, communities, countries and republics – we face a situation that game theory calls the *prisoner's dilemma*.[64] The prisoner knows that if he cooperates with another prisoner, the outcome will be better than if he had acted on his own. However, if he places his trust in the other prisoner, who then betrays him, then it is the traitor who will carry off the spoils and he will be left with nothing. The outcome will be far worse for him than if he had acted alone. A bad outcome can only be countered by distrusting the trust of the other and pursuing one's own profit, even if said profit will be lower than would result from cooperation.

And so according to game theory, any cooperation requiring trust is irrational – if, that is, we regard the decision-making situation as unique and isolated. There is no error. The process of sociogenesis must have been created by nature at the level of the family by

---

64 The prisoner's dilemma as a problem of collective action has been known since Rousseau. It was given its name by Albert W. Tucker. Two prisoners commit a crime. In order to coax a confession from them, the judge makes the following offer: if both confess, they will be sentenced to five years; if neither confesses, each will receive a two-year sentence. But if only one confesses to the crime, then he will be released and the other will receive ten years. In summary:

		Second prisoner	
		confesses	does not confess
First	confesses	5/5	0/10
prisoner	does not confess	10/0	2/2

where in first place in the case of each variant of confession of the first prisoner is the number of years he would be sentenced to, and in second place the number of years for the second prisoner. Each prisoner would, it goes without saying, rather do two years than five. Regardless of the behaviour of the second, the first will receive a better outcome if he confesses to everything: five years instead of ten if the second also confesses, released immediately instead of in two years if the second does not confess. The second prisoner also knows that he will receive a better outcome if he confesses. And the first knows that the second knows this. So it is a better move for both to confess, even though if neither confessed, they would each be sentenced to only two years.

implanting in our genes the basic capital of trust in blood ties and amorous irrationality for the establishment of new bonds.

For the emergence of larger societies, rationality thus operated on a higher level than that of the decision-making of game theory, namely, the rationality of history. It works slowly, but answers the prisoner's dilemma by repeating it indefinitely. Since an infinite sum of even small punishments is greater than a single large punishment, which necessarily has to be risked in order to answer the dilemma, sociogenesis is logical and human solidarity is possible and rational. Europe has a long history of overcoming mistrust: from the level of fortified households to that of family clans and clients, thence to the level of fortified communities, and finally to the level of fortified states that are today being integrated into the European community, overcoming mistrust at a level that is for us a desired goal.

Our newly acquired freedom will not help us if we are unable to get rid of old superstitions. For several generations we have been told that in capitalism *homo homini lupus est*. That it is the society of the contract, in which what is written is given, and the rest is of no interest. When it comes to business, you owe your brother no favours. So now we have capitalism... And lo and behold! Everything is different. Just as under the old regime it was important and difficult to live by the slogan *Live in truth!*, so, it seems to me, it is now becoming more and important to live by the axiom *Trust others!*

Things are not likely to get any easier.

Wassenaar, January 1991

BIBLIOGRAPHY

Abalkin, L.: Interview in *Ogoňok*, 1989, No. 13.

Arendt, H.: *The Origins of Totalitarianism*. London: Allen & Unwin 1958.

Ash, T. G.: *We the People: the Revolution of 68 Witnessed in Warsaw, Budapest and Prague*. Cambridge: Granada Books 1990.

Ben-Porath, Y.: The F -connection: Families, Friends and Firms. *Population and Development Review*, 1980, 6, 1–30.

Berger, P. L.: Morální úvaha a politický čin. *Tvorba* 7. 2. 1990.

Bourdieu, P.: *Outline of a Theory of Practice*. Cambridge: Cambridge University Press 1977.

Cohen, P. S.: *Modern Social Theory*. London: Heineman 1968.

Coleman, J. S.: Social Capital in the Creation of Human Capital. *American Journal of Sociology*, 94, 1988, 95–120.

Collins, R.: *Conflict Sociology. Toward an Explanatory Science*. New York: Academic Press 1975.

Dahrendorf, R.: *The Modern Social Conflict*. London: Weidenfeld and Nicholson 1988.

Djilas, M.: *The New Class: An Analysis of the Communist System*. London: Thames & Hudson 1957.

Durkheim, E.: L'individualisme et les intellectuels. *Revue Bleu*, vol. 4, no. 10 (1898), 7–13. Quoted from R. N. Bellah (ed.): *Emile Durkheim on Morality and Society*. Chicago: University of Chicago Press 1973.

Durkheim, E.: *Montesquieu et Rousseau précurseurs de la sociologie*. Paris: Riviére 1953.

Gouldner, A. W.: *The Future of Intellectuals and the Rise of the New Class*. London: MacMillan 1979.

Granovetter, M.: Economic Action, Social Structure, and Embeddedness. *American Journal of Sociology*, 91, 1985, 481–510.

Habermas, J.: Toward a Theory of Communicative Competence. In: *Recent Sociology* No. 2, ed. H. P. Dreitzel. New York: The MacMillan Company 1970.

Habermas, J.: *Knowledge and Human Interests*. Boston: Beacon Press 1971.

Habermas, J.: *Communication and the Evolution of Society*. Boston: Beacon Press 1979.

Inglehart, R.: *Culture Shift in Advanced Industrial Society*. Princeton: Princeton University Press 1990.

Jordan, B., M. Redley, S. James: *Putting the Family First.* London: UCL Press 1994.

Keller, J.: Problém moci u Giddense a Colemana. *Sociologický časopis,* 1990, 5.

Klofáč, J., V. Tlustý: *Soudobá sociologie.* Praha: NPL 1965.

Kornai, J.: *Economics of Shortage.* London: Elsevier 1981.

Mauss, M.: *The Gift.* London: Allen & Unwin 1966.

Mount, F.: *The Subversive Family.* London: Jonathan Cape 1982.

Možný, I.: O rodině. In: *Socialistický životní způsob jako sociální realita.* Brno: FF UJEP 1982. (conference proceedings) Reprinted in I. Možný: *Moderní rodina: mýty a skutečnosti.* Brno: Blok 1990.

Nora, P. et al., *Les lieux de mémoire,* vols. 1–3. Paris: Gallimard 1997.

Petrusek, M.: *Princip komplementarity a problém tolerance v sociologii.* Bratislava 1986, mimeographed.

Petrusek, M. (pseud. Polehňa Jan): Ještě jednou o třídách za socialismu aneb jak je krásné býti kadeřavým. *Sociologický obzor,* Vol. 1 (1987), No. 4 (samizdat).

Petrusek, M. (pseud. Polehňa Jan): Teorie sociální exkluze a naše reality. *Sociologický obzor,* Vol. 2 (1988), No. 2 (samizdat).

Petrusek, M.: Koncepce kulturního kapitálu v soudobé západní sociologii. (Intelektuálové, třídy a symbolická dominance.) In: *Soudobá teoretická sociologie na západě.* Praha: Ústav pro filozofii a sociologii ČSAV 1989.

Pithart, P.: Pokus o vlast: Bolzano, Rádl, Patočka a my v roce 1979. *Svědectví,* 59 (1979).

Pithart, P.: Odvahu myslet. *Listy,* April 1980, 35–40.

Pithart, P.: *Dějiny a politika.* Praha: Prostor 1990.

Polanyi, K.: *The Great Transformation.* New York: Rinehart 1944.

Polanyi, K.: *Primitive, Archaic and Modern Economy.* Ed. George Dalton. New York: Doubleday 1968.

Potůček, M., S. Szomolányiová (eds.): *Funkcionální analýza v sociologii.* Praha: Čs. sociologická společnost 1989, mimeographed.

Rabušic, L.: Roots and Elements of 1989 Revolution in Czechoslovakia. *Proceedings of IV World Congress for Soviet and East European Studies.* Harrogate 1990.

Rabušic, L., P. Mareš, L. Musil: Social Change in Perception of Czech Population One Year after Revolution. *Proceedings of Conference Social Change and Macroplanning.* Dubrovnik: IUC 1991.

Ringen, S.: *Citizens, Families, and Reform.* Oxford: Clarendon Press 1997.

Ruml, J.: Hra s čísly. *Lidové noviny*, 1989 (Vol. 2), No. 11 (samizdat). Reprinted in: *Lidové noviny II*. Praha: SNTL 1990 (unpag.).

Runciman, W. G.: *A Treatise on Social Theory II: Substantive Social Theory*. Cambridge: Cambridge University Press 1989.

Russell, B.: *Power: A New Social Analysis*. London: Allen & Unwin 1938.

Szelenyi, I.: Strategie a důsledky přechodu od redistributivní ke smíšené hospodářské soustavě. Public lecture in SoÚ ČSAV and dept. of sociology FF MU, March 1990.

Tiger, L., R. Fox: *The Imperial Animal*. New York: Holt, Rinehart & Winston 1971.

Tyszka, Z.: *Socjologia rodziny*. Warszawa: PWN 1974.

Vaculík, L.: Speech at the 4th conference of the Czechoslovak Writers Union. In: *Spisovatelé a moc*. Praha: Čs. spisovatel 1968.

Wellman, B., S. D. Berkowitz (eds.): *Social Structures. A Network Approach*. Cambridge: Cambridge University Press 1988.

Wiener, N.: *Kybernetika a společnost*. Praha: Nakladatelství ČSAV 1963.

The **Václav Havel Series** aims to honor and extend the intellectual legacy of the dissident, playwright, philosopher, and president whose name it proudly bears. Prepared with Ivan M. Havel, and other personalities and institutions closely associated with Václav Havel, such as the Václav Havel Library and Forum 2000, the series focuses on modern thought and the contemporary world – encompassing history, politics, art, architecture, and ethics. While the works often concern the Central European experience, the series – like Havel himself – focuses on issues that affect humanity across the globe.

Published titles
Jiří Přibáň, *The Defence of Constitutionalism: The Czech Question in Postnational Europe*
Matěj Spurný, *Making the Most of Tomorrow: A Laboratory of Socialist Modernity in Czechoslovakia*
Jacques Rossi, *Fragmented Lives: Chronicles of the Gulag*
Jiří Přibáň & Karel Hvížďala, *In Quest of History: On Czech Statehood and Identity*
Miroslav Petříček, *Philosophy en noir: Rethinking Philosophy after the Holocaust*
Petr Roubal, *Spartakiads: The Politics of Physical Culture in Communist Czechoslovakia*
Josef Šafařík, *Letters to Melin: A Discourse on Science and Progress*
Martin C. Putna, *Rus - Ukraine - Russia: Scenes from the Cultural History of Russian Religiosity*
Ivo Možný, *Why So Easily ... Some Family Reasons for the Velvet Revolution*

Forthcoming
Kieran Williams – David Danaher (eds), *Václav Havel's Meanings: His Key Words and Their Legacy*
Marie Černá, *The Soviet Army and Czech Society 1968-1989*
Olivier Mongin, *The Urban Condition: The City in a Globalizing World*
Ivan M. Havel et al., *Letters from Olga*